SPIRITUAL WARFARE FOR WOMEN

Spiritual Warfare for Women

Leighann McCoy

Bethany House Publishers
a division of Baker Publishing Group
Minneapolis, Minnesota

Published by Bethany House Publishers
11400 Hampshire Avenue South
Bloomington, Minnesota 55438
www.bethanyhouse.com

Bethany House Publishers is a division of
Baker Publishing Group, Grand Rapids, Michigan

Printed in the United States of America

Library of Congress Cataloging-in-Publication Data

McCoy, Leighann.
Spiritual warfare for women : winning the battle for your home, family, and friends / Leighann McCoy.
p. cm.
Summary: "Author and women's conference leader examines spiritual warfare for a specifically female audience"—Provided by publisher.
Includes bibliographical references (p.).
ISBN 978-0-7642-0890-4 (pbk. : alk. paper)
1. Christian women—Religious life. 2. Spiritual warfare. I. Title.
BV4527.M373 2011
235′.4082—dc23 2011019417

Emphasis in Scripture shown by italics is the author's.

Cover design by Koechel Peterson & Associates, Inc., Minneapolis, Minnesota.

Author is represented by Smith Management Partners, LLC.

In keeping with biblical principles of creation stewardship, Baker Publishing Group advocates the responsible use of our natural resources. As a member of the Green Press Initiative, our company uses recycled paper when possible. The text paper of this book is composed in part of post-consumer waste.

15 16 17 18 19 20 11 10 9 8 7 6

Dedicated to

Lounette Keesee, my mother

*You've taught me how to "fight the good fight"
through the example of your life.*

Contents

Foreword

Churches are dividing; parents are divorcing; children are rebelling; gambling, sexual, and chemical addictions are rampant; and the Christian community is experiencing a blues epidemic in an age of anxiety. Could the devil and his angels have anything to do with this mayhem?

Every conservative theologian acknowledges that "our struggle is not against flesh and blood, but against the rulers, against the authorities, against the powers of this dark world and against the spiritual forces of evil in the heavenly realm" (Ephesians 6:12). Jesus referred to Satan as the ruler or prince of this world (John 12:31; 16:11). The apostle John wrote, "The whole world is under the control of the evil one" (1 John 5:19). The real question is how a disarmed enemy can have such worldwide influence, and in what way are we vulnerable?

The fact that we are vulnerable is revealed in the High Priestly Prayer. Jesus is about to remove His physical presence from planet earth and leave behind His eleven disciples. One of His disciples was no longer with Him, because "the devil had already put into the heart of Judas Iscariot, Simon's son, to betray him, Jesus" (John 13:2

ESV). Knowing what His disciples would have to face, Jesus prays, "My prayer is not that you take them out of the world but that you protect them from the evil one. They are not of the world, even as I am not of it. Sanctify them by the truth; your word is truth. As you sent me into the world, I have sent them into the world. For them I sanctify myself, that they too may be truly sanctified. My prayer is not for them alone. I pray also for those who will believe in me through their message" (John 17:15–20).

The first concern of our Lord is that we be kept from the evil one, and being sanctified in truth is the means by which that can happen. The only way to overcome the Father of Lies is to know the truth, and knowing the truth will set us free (John 8:32). The belt of truth is the first piece of our armor, which is our protection against the deceiver. Satan's schemes haven't changed much from when he first appeared in the garden of Eden. Eve was deceived and she believed a lie. The breastplate of righteousness is the next piece of armor; it is our protection against the accuser. When we put on the armor of God, we are actually putting on the Lord Jesus Christ, who is the Truth, and we are saved by His righteousness. The only real sanctuary we have is our identity and position in Christ.

The apostle Paul has penned a sober warning concerning the times in which we live: "The Spirit clearly says that in later times some will abandon the faith and follow deceiving spirits and things taught by demons" (1 Timothy 4:1). That is presently happening all over the world. I have personally counseled hundreds and hundreds of Christians who are struggling with tempting, accusing, condemning, and blasphemous thoughts. In the vast majority of cases, that battle for their mind has proven to be spiritual. Based on 2 Timothy 2:24–26, we have learned how to help these dear people resolve their personal and spiritual conflicts through genuine repentance and faith in God. In the process they are submitting to God and resisting the devil (James 4:7). Most experience for the first time the peace of God guarding their hearts and their minds in Christ Jesus (Philippians 4:6–7).

Satan can't do anything about our identity and position in Christ, but if he can deceive us into believing that it isn't true, we will live as though it isn't. If the Enemy can invade your mind undetected and get you to believe a lie, he could negatively influence your life, and that will affect your marriage, family, and ministry. That is why the apostle Paul admonishes us to take every thought captive to the obedience of Christ (2 Corinthians 10:5).

My friends Tom and Leighann McCoy have a very fruitful ministry. Tom pastors one of the fastest growing churches in middle Tennessee, and Leighann directs the women's and prayer ministries. They are not ignorant of Satan's schemes. Leighann has written a biblically solid and practical book that will be a blessing to the church, and especially helpful for women. She has fought the good fight and wisely instructs others how to stand firm in their faith.

DR. NEIL T. ANDERSON

FOUNDER AND PRESIDENT EMERITUS
OF FREEDOM IN CHRIST MINISTRIES

Acknowledgments

No writer writes alone. A special thank-you to these who have participated in the production of this book:

Ron Smith, my manager, and Bethany House Publishers, who have chosen to believe in me and invest in my work.

Thompson Station Church. You have been God's hands and feet to me and my family for over twenty years and especially in 2010. I'm especially grateful to our pastors who fight alongside us and who are praying us through. I'm grateful too for our ministry assistants who not only pray for us but also read my manuscripts "one last time." I'm grateful for the seven Connect Groups who have committed to pray each day of the week for my family and for the SELAH women who heard these messages first. A special thank-you also goes to Jennifer Houston (and Kim), who typed my entire manuscript when we lost it in the computer.

My prayer partners. These seven women pray with me, wash my feet, give me Scripture, and buy me PJs. I want to say a special thank-you to my friend Kathleen Carney, who literally held me together in my darkest hour (don't forget to be grateful for your carrot cake); and my children's "other mother," Terra Tucker. Also a special "I love you, and what would I do without you?" to my prayer partner in life and ministry, Karen Philpott. Thank you also to my prayer partners at Lifeway Christian Resources, Chris Adams and the Lifeway women's ministry staff, and especially the Ministry Multipliers—just knowing you are out there means the world to me. I especially want to thank my own LMM prayer partner Sheila West—for being with me "for such a time as this."

Dr. Max Caudill and Dr. Alan Herline. These are the physicians who ministered healing to me in my battle against cancer. They made being sick a tiny bit easier. I'm grateful also for Dr. Ruth Lamar, my oncologist, who continues to walk with me now.

Tom, Mikel, Kaleigh, and TJ—I hope you know that you mean the world to me. I know that you are happier than I am that this book is done. Thank you for following hard after God's best for your lives.

To God be the glory!

Introduction

I almost didn't write this book for fear I'd be under such attack from the Enemy that I wouldn't be able to survive it. But then I realized that's the exact reason I had to write.

I grew up in a denomination that taught me very little about spiritual warfare. If ever I asked about the reality of spiritual warfare, the adults in my world raised their eyebrows, drew me close, and whispered, "We just don't talk about things like that." I wondered why we were whispering.

Because little was said and even less was taught, I adopted my own theology of spiritual warfare. It went something like this: What you don't know can't hurt you. Only people who are a bit wacky want to get involved in that kind of thing. And, just don't go there.

But after twenty-plus years as a pastor's wife, many of those spent in discovering the incredible power of prayer, my theology of spiritual warfare has proven to be not only wrong but grossly false. In fact, I've come to realize that the exact opposite is true: What you don't know about spiritual warfare most certainly *can* hurt you—even more because it catches you off guard. People who are reasonably sane are also targeted for attack. In fact, I discovered that the best qualifier for spiritual attack is simply being naïve enough to start taking God at His Word. And as far as going there, you don't have to. The Enemy is aggressive and he'll bring the battle to you.

Then God gave me the opportunity to sit under the teaching of Dr. Neil Anderson (Freedom in Christ Ministries). Dr. Anderson is a theologian, a pastoral counselor, and a world-renowned teacher. Just the fact that I was having lunch with him at Chili's across the street from the Williamson Memorial Gardens was amazing enough. But as we ate, my husband and I listened to Dr. Anderson ramble. And when Dr. Anderson rambles he says more than most people say when they deliver well-prepared messages. In the midst of his rambling, he asked us this question: "Wouldn't it make sense that we truly worship that which we most fear?"

I thought for a moment and agreed. Yes, it does make sense that what we fear most we worship. Our fear drives us to adjust our behavior so that we honor the object of our fear. I nodded in agreement and thought of the people in India who feared Shiva—the god of curses personified in the form of a blue snake. They brought Shiva gifts, bowed down before idols of Shiva, placed this image of Shiva in their homes, and wrapped Shiva around their necks. The Hindu people in India worshiped Shiva out of fear.

As I was thinking of Shiva, Dr. Anderson brought his point home with this: "Many Christians fear Satan more than God."

Wham.

Ever have that happen to you? It takes the wind out of your sails, doesn't it? Makes you want to sit down and try to shake the impact. Do I fear Satan more than I fear God?

Just as I was trying to wrestle with the thought, he continued, "And that which you fear most becomes a god to you."

Images of idol worship came to my mind. And suddenly I realized that in avoiding the subject of spiritual warfare, I had inadvertently become a worshiper of idols. I had allowed my fear of the Enemy to supersede my worship of God. I was guilty of allowing my fear to drive me to "worship" a lesser god.

So I'm writing this book. I'm writing this book because I am not afraid. I'm writing this book because you shouldn't be either. I'm writing this book because women have lived far too long battered about by an unknown foe. I'm writing this book because I'm tired of standing far from the action, merely bandaging the wounded.

I wrote that part of my introduction in February. On March 1 I was diagnosed with colon cancer. On May 1 our church was flooded (when middle Tennessee experienced rainfall of "biblical proportions"), causing $275,000 worth of damage to our worship center and children's classrooms. And on May 31 my firstborn daughter (age eighteen, just graduated from high school) moved out of our home and into a tiny apartment with her boyfriend, leaving behind numerous scholarships at a great Christian college. I found out on June 18 that she is pregnant. (As I write this, she doesn't even know that I know.)

Today is June 21 and I'm still writing this book. Why? Because I refuse to worship a lesser god. I believe more today than I even knew to believe in February that I serve a God who reigns. He alone is supreme; there is no other being in heaven, on earth, or under the earth that is more powerful than He. I am confident that as I write this book He will continue to prove himself faithful to His promises as He brings glory to himself in and through my life and the lives of those I love.

I'm still writing this book because I am convinced that He will do the same for you. God is God—and He will BE HIMSELF as He wins the battles in your life. I smile as I realize that He was not willing to let me lead you on this trek simply out of the battles I've already won. (Something I was more than willing to do.) Instead, in His sovereign wisdom, He chose to allow a mess that is current so that you would have a teacher from the trenches. I'm not a decorated war hero. I'm a soldier who's fighting as I write.

Now I'm faced with the challenge of sharing these powerful truths in a way that communicates them to you. I am a pushover for beautiful packages. I love a well-wrapped gift. When someone takes time to wrap a present and decorate it with a bow, they are saying, "I want to make you smile—and just you wait until you see what I've gotten for you!" I want my books to make you feel the same way. I especially want a book on spiritual warfare to be wrapped in such a way.

That is why I've organized my book in four parts. In part 1, I want to help you discover the incredible inexhaustible love of God. In part 2, I will expose the Enemy for who he is. This package might not seem as pretty as the first, but it will prove to be tremendously valuable to you (like the vacuum cleaner my thoughtful husband bought me one year for Christmas). In part 3, we will take a more in-depth look at the specific areas of a woman's life that the Enemy targets for attack: our marriages, children, friends, health, and churches. Then in part 4, I will show you how God has already equipped you to live triumphantly while you do some serious damage to the spiritual forces that dare to come your way.

Each chapter begins with a verse and concludes with a prayer. Throughout the book I have sprinkled fictional visits with biblical characters. I hope they will bring Scripture to life for you. Be sure to check my integrity by looking up the biblical references and reading the actual Scripture that inspired my imagination. Be careful to allow these fictional visits to serve as illustrations of truth—not truth themselves.

On the last page of each chapter you will also find a section called "Sharpen Your Sword." This includes a list of truths I've gleaned from God's Word and the Scripture verses that support those truths. Following those truths is a practical hint on how to commit God's Word to memory. The Word of God is your most powerful weapon against the Enemy. You will read more about that throughout this book and especially in chapter 13.

Jesus called Satan a liar. Satan is the worst kind of liar. He doesn't merely lie; he deceives by twisting and contaminating truth. Your best defense against the lies of the devil is the Word of God. When Jesus prayed for His disciples, He prayed, "My prayer is not that you take them out of the world but that you protect them from the evil one. . . . Sanctify them by the truth; your word is truth" (John 17:15, 17).

When you develop the spiritual discipline of Scripture memory, you develop the skill to use the sword of the Spirit, which is the Word of God. This one discipline will give you a great advantage in winning the battles you face.

My prayer is that as you read this book you will unwrap a powerful understanding of how much God loves you. For Scripture teaches us that "perfect love casts out fear" (1 John 4:18 ESV). I hope that as you learn to recognize the "schemes of the devil" you will grow in your ability to stand firm against him so that you might boldly advance God's kingdom on earth. I hope that you discover who you are in Christ, and what you are already equipped to do.

> Jesus loves me! This I know,
> For the Bible tells me so.
> Little ones to Him belong;
> They are weak, but He is strong.
>
> Yes, Jesus loves me!
> Yes, Jesus loves me!
> Yes, Jesus loves me!
> The Bible tells me so.[1]

And that's what spiritual warfare is really about. It's all about love. The warfare, the battle, the victories, and the defeats; they are all driven by God's relentless pursuit—fueled by His uncompromising love. God loves you. And in His love He's invited you to face your fear, for there is another who "loves you not."

What do you fear? What do you worship? Isn't it time you took your worship to a whole new level? Isn't it time to stop bowing to a lesser god? It is time for me! I want to start winning the battles for my home, family, and friends. Don't you? "You, dear children, are from God and have overcome them, because the one who is in you is greater than the one who is in the world" (1 John 4:4).

PART ONE

THE MOST POWERFUL WEAPON OF ALL —*the Love of God*

God has objectively defeated Satan and his agenda. He has delivered us from sin's penalty and power, and ultimately he will deliver us from sin's very presence. In the interim, we are involved in guerilla warfare with demonic forces.

As believers, we have been transferred from the kingdom of darkness to the kingdom of light, with all the rights, privileges, and position that being a child of God entails. The spiritual battle we fight involves a responsibility on our part to put on the spiritual protection that God has provided for us. We can and will resist the enemy's attempts to deceive, accuse, and cast doubt when we stand firm against him. . . . The great majority of spiritual warfare need never go beyond the regular practice of living out our position in Christ by faith.[1]

CHIP INGRAM, *THE INVISIBLE WAR*

Chapter One

God Is Love

> The Lord your God is with you, he is mighty to save. He will take great delight in you, he will quiet you with his love, he will rejoice over you with singing.
>
> Zephaniah 3:17

If you are reading this book because you want to learn more about spiritual warfare, you might be wondering why the first chapter begins with the love of God. We're starting here because this is where the battle begins; God loved us, and Satan didn't like it. In fact, you wouldn't even be reading this book if God didn't initiate a love relationship with you. You are reading this book right now because "he first loved us."

"We love because he first loved us." 1 John 4:19

As you learn to identify and embrace God's love, you will then be ready to learn more about your Enemy's ways. In fact, you do not have to be an excellent student of evil in order to avoid it. You simply need to develop an attraction for all things good. For when you do that, the mere hint of evil will become apparent (and disgusting) to you.

The best place to anchor your understanding of spiritual warfare is in the firm foundation of God's constant love. And God loved us first when He created us. So we will begin our discussion of God's love "in the beginning."

CREATED BY GOD

Scripture tells us that "in the beginning God created the heavens and the earth." I love how Genesis 1:1–2 sets the stage for the creation story:

> In the beginning God created the heavens and the earth. Now the earth was formless and empty, darkness was over the surface of the deep, and the Spirit of God was hovering over the waters.

That is the part I like, "the Spirit of God was hovering over the waters." Isn't that a powerful thought . . . the Spirit of God hovering? I can't help but wonder where the Spirit of God hovers today. However, Genesis 1:3–31 tells us that the Spirit of God didn't hover for long. The Word of God spoke and the Spirit of God created.

> "Let there be light," and there was light. . . .
>
> "Let there be an expanse between the waters to separate water from water." So God made the expanse and separated the water under the expanse from the water above it. And it was so. . . .
>
> "Let the water under the sky be gathered to one place, and let the dry land appear." And it was so.

You get the idea. God's *Word* created our world. Then, God's *Word* created us. But God did more than simply speak when He created man. God breathed his own breath into Adam and Eve. "The Lord God formed the man from the dust of the ground and *breathed into his nostrils the breath of life*, and the man became a living being" (Genesis 2:7).

Remember the hovering Spirit of God? The same Spirit that "hovered over the waters" breathed life into man. Life came from God. *Your* life came from the breath of God.

Now look at the sweet description of the creation of woman:

> The Lord God said, "It is not good for the man to be alone. I will make a helper suitable for him." Now the Lord God had formed out of the ground all the beasts of the field and all the birds of the air. He brought them to the man to see what he would name them; and whatever the man called each living creature, that was its name. So the man gave names to all the livestock, the birds of the air and all the beasts of the field. But for Adam no suitable helper was found. So the Lord God caused the man to fall into a deep sleep; and while he was sleeping, he took one of the man's ribs and closed up the place with flesh. Then the Lord God made a woman from the rib he had taken out of the man, and he brought her to the man. The man said, "This is now bone of my bones and flesh of my flesh; she shall be called 'woman,' for she was taken out of man."
>
> Genesis 2:18–23

Throughout the creation story everything was "good" until Genesis 2:18. And for the first time the Lord God declared one thing to be "not good." It was "not good" that we (women) had not been created. Isn't that great? Only after God created Eve did He finally rest and declare it all "very good."

God created man in His own image and then gave him dominion over the earth. It was as if God created all the rest (the birds of the air, beasts of the field, sun and moon, stars and water, fish and plants) to sustain and support His crown creations, us! David pondered this thought during his quiet time one day and penned Psalm 8. Read Psalm 8 and wonder with David at the love God has toward us.

God created us to love us. Genesis 1:28 and 2:15–17 paint us a picture of God's original design. God blessed Adam and Eve, encouraged them to have plenty of children, to rule over all the other living creatures, to take care of the garden of Eden, and to stay away from the Tree of Knowledge of Good and Evil. God told Adam that if he ate of that particular tree he would "surely die."

Can you imagine life in the garden? I can. In my imagination, everything there was perfect to sustain life. The fruits and vegetables grew in abundance without any blemishes or thorns or weeds. The temperature ranged between 72 and 80 degrees both day and night, the ground was soft like a "cloud nine" bed, and there was never any rain (or thunder, or torrential downpours that flood churches and homes, or tornadoes or hurricanes or snowstorms!). All Adam and Eve had to do was take care of the animals, feast on the food, and enjoy each other. Then in the cool of the day they took pleasure walks with God (Genesis 3:8).

Life was good in the garden, but not void of spiritual warfare.

SPIRITUAL WARFARE BEGAN IN THE GARDEN

Satan made his first appearance in the garden of Eden. Scripture doesn't give us much to buffer our understanding of the strange phenomenon of talking serpents. Genesis 3:1 almost implies that talking with the animals might have been common in the garden of Eden. But more significant than a serpent with a voice is the conversation that took place: "Did God say, 'You must not eat from any tree in the garden'?"

Satan took an interesting approach with Eve. Rather than speak truth or blatantly lie, he simply cast shadows of doubt. This is what he most often does. Satan rarely ever tells blatant lies when he initiates his conversations (although his native language is lying; see John 8:44). He usually uses a remnant of truth, then distorts it to plant a seed of doubt. Of course the distortion makes his statement a lie. And his cunning process of twisting truth leads to deception, which is far more dangerous than simple lies. You will see how this strategy unfolded for Adam and Eve in just a minute.

The serpent's question to Eve provoked an immediate response with an obvious answer.

> We may eat fruit from the trees in the garden, but God did say, "You must not eat fruit from the tree that is in the middle of the garden, and you must not touch it, or you will die."
>
> Genesis 3:2–3

Satan wasn't concerned with the answer to his question. He wanted to divert Eve's attention from what she could have and place it on the one thing she couldn't have: fruit from the tree in the middle of the garden. He still does this today: If you are married, God gave you your marriage so that you can enjoy all that life has to offer with deep intimacy and unashamed love in a blessed covenant relationship with your husband. You can enjoy everything intimate with him! But . . . did God really say you couldn't ever have an intimate relationship with any other man?

Because you are a woman, God gave you the unique gifting to nurture, love, and care tenderly for your family as you manage your home. You have the power to create an atmosphere that provides nourishment physically, emotionally, and spiritually for your family. But . . . did God really say you couldn't spend freely on credit cards to transform your home into a magazine picture? Wouldn't new furniture, window treatments, and stainless steel appliances meet the needs of your family?

These are just two examples of Satan's cunning lies. Advertising agencies charge top dollar to tap into our felt needs all day long. Their goal is to remind us of what we don't have and stir us up until we find ourselves in a place of dissatisfaction so that we'll spend money, time, energy, or effort on their clients' products or services. It's amazing what we are willing to give up when the Enemy focuses our attention on forbidden fruit.

Why did Satan start his conversation with Eve in this way? My imagination tells me that Adam sat Eve down, perhaps on the first day that they met, and explained to her God's instructions for life in the garden. He showed her all the plants and animals (he'd thoroughly toured the garden already), and shared with her his enthusiasm for his neighborhood. When their stomachs rumbled, he rushed over to his favorite fruit tree and chose for her the best fruit on the tree. Perhaps it was a tree-ripened mango. There is no other fruit that can rival fresh mango, in my opinion. As they ate their mangoes, Adam continued his tour—offering Eve a large leafy fern to wipe the juice that dripped from her chin. They came to the center of the garden, and Adam pointed to the forbidden tree. He said, "Eve, that's the one, the one God said to leave alone. Don't go near that tree. It's best to stay away from this part of the garden altogether. Then you won't accidentally pluck the fruit and eat it." Eve might have said, "The fruit looks good." And Adam might have responded, "Maybe it is, but we'll never know because we won't be eating from that tree." And with that they walked on by and continued to enjoy their mangoes.

When Satan questioned Eve, he knew God's rules, but he had to do something to attract her attention to the forbidden tree. As he spoke, he might have walked subtly toward the center of the garden. Eve most likely didn't even notice him move as she followed him there. With the tree in view, the serpent responded, "You will not surely die. . . . For God knows that when you eat of it your eyes will be opened, and you will be like God, knowing good and evil" (Genesis 3:4–5).

That is when he blatantly lied. Satan told Eve she would not die—and she did. He also told her that she would be more like God if she ate the fruit—and she wasn't. In fact, in her sinless state of life she was more like God than she was after she sinned. But in

The Lure of Satan

Satan is a liar! Jesus called him the Father of Lies.

> You belong to your father, the devil, and you want to carry out your father's desire. He was a murderer from the beginning, not holding to the truth, for there is no truth in him. When he lies, he speaks his native language, for he is a liar and the father of lies.
>
> John 8:44

Satan is a subtle liar. His motivation is deception. He longs to deceive you with half truths and shortcuts. We will discuss this later, but for now understand this powerful truth: Satan is a liar!

true form, Satan didn't tell an absolute lie; that would be too easy to identify. Instead he buffered his lies with a bit of truth: "Your eyes will be opened and [you will be] knowing good and evil." This was only partial truth, for Adam and Eve already knew good, they just didn't have anything to compare it to so they didn't know to call it good. But evil—Satan was right, Adam and Eve had no understanding of evil until after they ate the forbidden fruit.

THE GREAT DIVORCE

Scripture calls what happened next "the fall of man." But I like C. S. Lewis's description of it as "the great divorce." The moment Eve took Satan at his word and plucked the fruit from that tree was the moment she divorced God. Adam followed suit quickly thereafter. Even though he'd received specific instructions to never touch the fruit on the Tree of Knowledge of Good and Evil (Genesis 2:16–17),

Adam ate the fruit that Eve plucked and he too divorced God. Both Adam and Eve turned their backs on God's instruction and chose their own way over His. Sin is as simple as that. Satan will try to convince sinners that they were not to blame; he will try to cloud them with "stinkin' thinkin'." But the truth of the matter is this—sin is a personal choice to reject God's instructions and go your own way.

SIN AND SHAME

> Then the eyes of both of them were opened, and they realized that they were naked; so they sewed fig leaves together and made coverings for themselves.
>
> GENESIS 3:7

Sin brought immediate shame to Adam and Eve. I don't know how long they had been romping in the garden in their birthday suits, but prior to their decisions to divorce God, they were in complete harmony and oneness with Him. They lived in complete harmony with one another too! Not only did Adam and Eve live in intimate oneness with God and each other, but they also lived in perfect community with the beasts of the field, the birds of the air, the fish, and all other plant and animal life God created. They didn't need blankets at night or toothbrushes in the morning. They weren't concerned about their weight or their body mass index, their shoe size or blisters.

Genesis 2:25 is a powerful verse: "The man and his wife were both naked, and they felt no shame." The fact that Adam and Eve lived naked proved that they had no shame. Think about that for a moment. The two of them had such a relationship, not only with one another but also with God and all of His creation, that they experienced *no shame*.

The other night my husband and I took a walk. It was extremely warm and the air was thick—unusually hot and humid for June even in Tennessee. We were walking because we'd just heard that our daughter was pregnant. We needed to process our news. As we walked, the fireflies put on a great show in the pastures that line the street in front of our house. When we returned home we were the only ones there. Our son was out with a friend, our daughter Kaleigh was in Mexico on a mission trip, and Mikel . . . well, she was with her boyfriend. The day was just about done, and it was dark enough for me to say, "Do you think we could skinny-dip in the pool and get away with it?" Tom grinned at the idea (and more so that I was the one to come up with it) and told me he needed to check with TJ to see when he was coming home. So he said, "Go on in. I'll be right there after I text TJ." I was hot and sticky and in desperate need to do something wild and crazy, so I slipped out of my clothes and into the pool. About two seconds later Tom joined me. We were naked and we were not ashamed. That is intimacy.

Of course my adventurous spirit waned about fifteen minutes later, and I told Tom I needed to go in. Tom and I had just wrapped our towels around our naked selves when we heard a car in the driveway. I took off running. TJ came into the house. "Mom, can Mikala and Kaitlyn . . . MOM! What were you doing?! You and Dad were skinny-dipping! Uh-uh!" Can you imagine my fifteen-year-old's surprise when he caught his parents skinny-dipping?

When Adam and Eve ate the forbidden fruit, they were immediately ashamed. The intimacy they shared with each other, the oneness they experienced with God, the harmony they shared with all of God's creation was ruined. The harmony and oneness they had taken for granted was destroyed. When Adam and Eve divorced God, all of creation fell with them. Intimacy shattered and it would not be reestablished until Jesus came to earth thousands of years later and died on the cross. Notice that Jesus spoke of this very thing in His prayer the night before He died.

> I'm praying not only for them but also for those who will believe in me because of them and their witness about me. The goal

> is for all of them to become one heart and mind—just as you, Father, are in me and I in you, so they might be one heart and mind with us. Then the world might believe that you, in fact, sent me. The same glory you gave me, I gave them, so they'll be as unified and together as we are—I in them and you in me. Then they'll be mature in this oneness, and give the godless world evidence that you've sent me and loved them in the same way you've loved me.
>
> John 17:20–23 (The Message)

Praise God that the intimacy that was destroyed in the garden was restored at the cross.

But back to the "great divorce"—it was not long after Adam and Eve stitched together their fig leaves that they were confronted by God. God cursed the serpent, Eve, and Adam, and then explained the magnitude of their new reality (the only reality we have ever known). Read Genesis 3 and be reminded of what sin cost.

GOD HATES DIVORCE

God hates divorce. In fact, by Genesis 6:6 God was sorry He'd ever made us: "The Lord was grieved that he had made man on the earth, and his heart was filled with pain."

Sin gives birth to shame and pain. Don't ever forget that. Sin always comes with a price tag. Sin always costs more than you want to pay. But even in God's grief, He allowed His mercy to temper His justice. And rather than wipe out creation altogether, He partnered with Noah to save a remnant of His creation on a very large ark. And so, we are still today descendants of Adam and Eve, and then Noah—who spent many unimaginable days cooped up on a floating zoo.

Unlike most divorced couples I know, God never gave up on man. God never gives up on you! No matter how often you disobey Him, no matter how many times you disappoint Him, as long as you are living He will continue to initiate a relationship with you. Why? Simply because God loves you.

The Old Testament records God's initiative in establishing and maintaining a personal relationship with His fallen creation. Rather than turn His back on us or destroy us, God pursued us. This is what I call "the great pursuit."

THE GREAT PURSUIT

The great pursuit began with Abraham and culminated with Jesus. God made a promise to Abraham that He fulfilled in Jesus. While Abraham (then called Abram) was minding his own business, God called him to follow Him.

> The Lord had said to Abram, "Leave your country, your people and your father's household and go to the land I will show you. I will make you into a great nation and I will bless you; I will make your name great, and you will be a blessing. I will bless those who bless you, and whoever curses you I will curse; and all peoples on earth will be blessed through you."
>
> Genesis 12:1–3

Thus began God's personal interaction with Abraham and his descendants. What followed is an amazing love story filled with adventure and intrigue, scorned love and passionate reconciliations. The only constant is God's relentless pursuit that culminated in the birth, life, crucifixion, and resurrection of Jesus Christ. Matthew 1 traces the genealogy of Christ all the way back to Abraham, thus connecting the dots between God's promise to Abraham and His fulfillment of that promise in Jesus. John summed up the "great pursuit" in the introduction to his gospel.

> In the beginning was the Word, and the Word was with God, and the Word was God. He was with God in the beginning.

> Through him all things were made; without him nothing was made that has been made. In him was life, and that life was the light of men. The light shines in the darkness, but the darkness has not understood it.
>
> JOHN 1:1–5

> The Word became flesh and made his dwelling among us. We have seen his glory, the glory of the One and Only, who came from the Father, full of grace and truth.
>
> JOHN 1:14

From the very beginning God put His plan in motion. The "great pursuit" continues today.

> For God so loved the world that he gave his one and only Son, that whoever believes in him shall not perish but have eternal life.
>
> JOHN 3:16

THE GREAT PURSUIT AS SEEN IN THE LIFE OF SARAH

Now that we've spent time with Adam and Eve and have been reminded of the impact of the "great divorce," let's go on a fictional visit with Sarah, who followed Abraham at the beginning of God's "great pursuit." She was a woman who experienced God's love in the midst of spiritual darkness.

Sarah was the wife of Abraham. When God initiated his relationship with Abraham, his name was Abram and Sarah's name was Sarai. I think it is interesting how Abram and Sarai's names were changed as they grew in their knowledge of God and as they experienced His activity in their lives. Sometimes I think God should change my name too.

When God called Abram to go to the elusive "land I will show you," Sarai went with him. In the following story you will hear how God's love might have penetrated Sarah's heart.

"Isaac! Put that little lamb down! You are going to break his leg!" Sarah reprimanded little Isaac as he set the terrified lamb on the ground. She took a deep breath and rested her head on the pole that held the tent in place. Her gray hair pressed against the dark canvas as a reminder of her age and Isaac's miracle birth.

She was sharing her story with Adah, a curious young woman who'd heard of the old couple and their miracle baby. Adah met Sarah at the well this morning and traveled home with her to hear her tell her story. "You were telling me how you knew, I mean really *knew* God loved you," Adah politely prompted Sarah to continue her story.

"Oh yes. Well, I didn't understand God's love for many years. I mean, what was Abram thinking? He just popped in one day and said, 'Sarai, we're following God to a land He will show us. Pack your things; we're leaving in the morning.' What would you have done?" Sarah's eyes sparkled as she lifted her head, leaned forward with excitement shining in her gaze, and challenged Adah with the question.

"I, uh, I don't know. I guess I would have packed, but who ever heard of going to a 'land that God would show them?' " Adah admitted how hard that must have been.

Sarah nodded. "Exactly. I packed and we went. Then along the way Abram started telling me the other things God told him. He said God promised to make him into a great nation. He said that God was going to bless him with so many children that he wouldn't be able to count them. He told me to look at the stars and then to look at the grains of sand. He said that God said we would have more children than even those."

Adah grinned. It was apparent that Isaac would most likely be Sarah's only child. For she was *old*, and to have him at such an old age had to be more than most women could handle. While Adah glanced at Isaac, Sarah interrupted her thoughts.

"Adah, don't you see how old I am?" Sarah smiled and Adah nodded—she was thinking that very thing.

"Why was God heckling and teasing my husband? What was He thinking?! Abram even told me that God changed his name from Abram to Abraham, 'father of a multitude,' and that He changed my name from Sarai to Sarah, 'princess.' Here God was promising Abraham that He would bless the entire world from my Abraham's descendants, and then that same God allowed me to be infertile!" The deep longing and heartache of infertility that Sarah had experienced for years rose up in her voice as she spoke.

Suddenly a kindred emotion kindled in Adah. She and Naphtali had been married for five years and also had yet to conceive a child. Adah remembered how she felt just last month when, after praying desperately for a baby, she was bombarded by those familiar cramps, and even on this day she was fully aware of the desperate void in her own barren womb.

"I'm afraid I would have thought the same thing," Adah said softly.

"Yes, well, I was foolish not to believe and I made a royal mess of things. When I laughed aloud at God's angels (they came for a visit one day just to encourage Abraham that God was going to make good on His promise), I thought for sure the Lord would strike me dead. I was so ashamed that they heard me. But, amazingly enough, God just smiled and declared that He would have the last laugh. He said that He and the entire world would laugh with me when He fulfilled every promise He ever made to Abraham." Sarah winked at Adah and they both chuckled.

"So when did you know God loved *you*?" Adah asked. Her own heart was filled with renewed hope that God would give her a son too.

"When Isaac first moved in my womb." Sarah smiled. "I was old! I mean, really old. My monthly cycles had ended long ago.

I dreamt of carrying a child for so many years and I'd imagined what it would feel like. But in all my imagination, I cannot tell you how different it really felt when it actually happened to me. The first time I sensed the flutter of his life in me, I knew God was the one true God and the Lord of Lords. I knew that no matter how impossible His promises might seem, He would be faithful to fulfill each and every one. I bowed down and worshiped God. Even with Isaac moving in my womb, I pressed my head to the ground and half expected God to chastise me for my unbelief, but instead He covered me with love. God's love felt like prickles on my skin and warmth in my soul. From that moment on, I understood the love of God." Tears welled in Sarah's eyes as she rubbed her tummy and glanced over toward Isaac, who was sitting in the dirt sorting pebbles.

"Let me rephrase that. I'm not sure I'll ever *understand* the love of God. But that was when I experienced it." Sarah smiled and Adah laughed.

GOD IS LOVE

Perhaps you are like Sarah. You've watched as others have spoken of having a personal relationship with God. They tell you how He speaks to them, directs them, and gives them encouragement when life becomes difficult. But, like Sarah, you just don't "get it." You read the Bible and hear the promises but they don't seem to apply to you.

I had a very close relative say to me once, "Leighann, God just doesn't work that way in my life." She was referring to the way I'd encouraged her to trust Him to bring good out of her suffering. She went on to say, "You're His favorite!"

Do you sometimes feel like God has played favorites and you're not one of them? Sarah could have very well felt that same way. She watched her husband live his life led by God, but until she actually conceived Isaac, she had a hard time believing in a God of promises. However, the day came in Sarah's life when God made good on His promise. And Sarah was just one of many women whose personal experiences with the love of God are chronicled in the Old Testament. If you've never read the stories of these women's lives, I challenge you to do so. Read of Rahab, Ruth, Gomer, and Esther. As you read their stories, see if you can find the many references to God's love for them. Study the dynamics of the way God interacted with them, and see if you can trace the path of His "great pursuit." I guarantee that God is pursuing you too. He *does* play favorites and He chose you! The Old Testament is filled with many other stories taken from the lives of both men and women who were chosen by God to partner with Him in His kingdom plan. Although Scripture has been canonized, and the whole of God's Word has been bound into sixty-six books, that doesn't mean you and I can't play a significant role in His world today. As you allow God to love you, the story of His love continues to be written. God still works through people and He still loves the world. God loves you—and He created you to receive His love. We are most human when we rest in this truth.

God Is Love

Read Hosea 2:14–20 aloud. Ask God to show you the ways He allures you today. Thank Him for each of these ways that He actively loves you today. (You might consider how He provides for you. How He gives you much more than you need. How He opens doors of ministry for you. How He never tires of hearing you ask for forgiveness.)

Think of ways God has been a husband to you. Thank Him for loving you.

Think of how God has "betrothed" you to himself. Thank Him for His love and compassion. Consider the love of God as demonstrated in the life, death, and resurrection of Jesus.

How might you acknowledge God today?

Begin your prayer with this:

Father, I know that I divorced you. I was born with the sinful nature passed down to me from Adam and Eve. And then when I was old enough to choose, I chose to sin. Even now I choose my own way over yours and fall far short of your plans for my life. Please forgive me for this. I long to experience your love. I want to be a woman of victory. I want to rise above the circumstances and walk in such a way that I bring glory to your Name. I love you, Lord, because you first loved me. Thank you for loving me.

SHARPEN YOUR SWORD

God loved us first. 1 John 4:19

Your life came from the breath of God. Genesis 2:7

God will always tell you the truth. Isaiah 45:19; John 8:32; 14:6; 16:13

God loves you and He created you to receive His love. You are most human when you rest in that truth. Psalms 36:5, 7; 63:3; and 86:13

Commit the Word to memory: Choose one of the verses mentioned above and print it on an index card. Print the verse on one side and the reference on the other. Carry your index card with you wherever you go. Pull it out when you are waiting for the doctor, the cashier, or your children. Read the verse aloud five times each time you look at your card. Then practice saying the verse without looking at your card.

Chapter Two

What Love Does

> "Though the mountains be shaken and the hills be removed, yet my unfailing love for you will not be shaken nor my covenant of peace be removed," says the Lord, who has compassion on you.
>
> Isaiah 54:10

If you attended a Southern Baptist church in the late 1970s, you might remember the musical *It's Cool in the Furnace*. I'll never forget it. My favorite song went like this (wish you could hear the tune):

> Shadrach, Meshach, Abednego . . .
> They had funny names and they lived far away
> but they set an example we can follow today.[1]

Another great song in that musical had this phrase: "It isn't HOT in the furnace, man; it isn't hot in the furnace, no that furnace is cool, cool, cool, cool." When we performed the musical at First Baptist Church, a college student named Ken played the role of cruel King Nebuchadnezzar. His performance was worthy of Oscar recognition. I'll never forget the night he got so "angry" that he shook his turban right off his head. The story about three men and a blazing furnace is recorded in the book of Daniel, and it illustrates what God's love does in the lives of His servants. This story provides scriptural basis for a powerful truth I challenge you to embrace today.

Every attack from the Enemy brings with it a divine invitation from the sovereign hand of God to learn by experience what love does.

If I did not believe that truth, I wouldn't be writing this book. I told you in the introduction that since I started writing I have been diagnosed with cancer, our church was flooded, and my daughter left home. What I have experienced may be more than what you have experienced in the past few months or less than what you have experienced recently. As I reference my personal battles, please know that in no way am I diminishing the battles you face. I am humble as I share with you that already I have experienced the love of God in each of these situations. Two of them (the cancer and flood) have impressively demonstrated the power and glory of God. And I am fully convinced that He will do the same, perhaps even bigger and better, in my daughter's life as well. Furthermore, I am convinced that God will also demonstrate His power and His glory in whatever circumstances you find yourself today.

Every attack from the Enemy—*every* one—brings with it a divine invitation to experience what God's love does. Romans 8:28 speaks this truth: "We know that *all things* work together for the good of those who love God: those who are called according to His purpose" (HCSB).

Notice that this verse says that *all things* work together for good. All things includes cancer, diabetes, fibromyalgia, Alzheimer's, divorce, affairs, husbands addicted to pornography, floods, tornadoes, fires, wars, prodigal children, depression, and anything else that invades your life to steal your joy. All things includes . . . ALL THINGS.

CHOICE SERVANTS OF GOD

The story of the fiery furnace illustrates this truth. Who were Shadrach, Meshach, and Abednego? How did they capture the attention of the king? What caused them to find themselves in a fiery furnace? In order to answer these questions, we need to begin in Daniel 1.

Nebuchadnezzar, king of Babylon, defeated Jehoiakim, king of Judah. He then ordered Ashpenaz, chief of his court officials, to select Israelites from the royal family to come live in the king's palace and participate in a training program. Nebuchadnezzar planned to give these men leadership in his kingdom once their training was complete. Daniel, Shadrach, Meshach, and Abednego were part of the elite group chosen to participate in Nebuchadnezzar's training plan.

All those chosen were young men, handsome, physically fit. They demonstrated great potential and were smart, wise, and capable of leadership (see Daniel 1:4). But our boys were even better than that. They rose to the top of the class. They were the cream of the crop. God gave them more knowledge and more understanding. Daniel even had the supernatural ability to interpret dreams. The king found none equal to them, and they proved wiser than all his other magicians and enchanters (see Daniel 1:19–20).

CHOICE SERVANTS OF GOD SET THEMSELVES APART FROM OTHERS

Daniel, Shadrach, Meshach, and Abednego set themselves apart from the others when they refused to compromise their faith. Daniel requested a special diet of vegetables and water for himself and his friends because they didn't want to "defile themselves" with the royal food and wine (Daniel 1:8, 11–16). At the risk of offending their captors, they requested special treatment. Just because they'd been taken captive didn't mean they were prepared to give up their devotion to God. A determination to serve the Lord almost always requires us to set ourselves apart from others. In fact, it was this determination to continue serving the Lord faithfully that got them all in trouble.

Spiritual battles often come our way because we are determined to serve the Lord. One of the truths I've learned about spiritual warfare is that the best way to assure you'll be attacked is to begin to take God at His Word. When you begin to trust God's Word—when you get serious about discipleship, when you decide to live a life of radical obedience directed by faith in God—you can count on spiritual attack. Jesus warned His disciples it would be this way:

> If the world hates you, keep in mind that it hated me first. If you belonged to the world, it would love you as its own. As it is, you do not belong to the world. That is why the world hates you. Remember the words I spoke to you: "No servant is greater than his master." If they persecuted me, they will persecute you also.
>
> John 15:18–20

A SERIOUS WARNING

I taught much of this book at my church this past spring. And on the first night of the study, I shared with the women most of what I wrote to you in my introduction. I confessed my fear and assured them that if they were attending this study in order to find a way to avoid spiritual warfare, they'd better not come back next week. I told them that throughout the course of study they'd most likely start experiencing more attack than ever before. My words proved to be true in my life—and so I give you the same warning right now. You're in chapter 2. If you are afraid, if your goal is to avoid

The Goal of the Christian Life

The goal of the Christian walk is not to avoid pain and suffering. Pain and suffering are guaranteed when we follow Jesus (John 16:33). Pain and suffering are also guaranteed if you don't follow Jesus. They are natural by-products of living in a sin-stained world (Genesis 3).

Many followers of Christ have wrapped their hearts around the deception that if they live right and do enough good they might earn the "right" to expect God to deliver them lives full of happiness and safety in return. And while many disciples do experience relatively safe and happy lives, many others experience lives filled with suffering and pain.

The goal of the Christian walk is to walk with Jesus through both the good times and the bad. God's intent is not to seal us up in a spiritually sterile bubble, but rather to allow the pain and suffering in this world to hammer and mold us into the image of His Son.

warfare at all cost, then put this book down. Don't read another word. I am warning you right now that your awareness of spiritual warfare will increase the more you learn about God and the more you seek to know Him intimately. The devil aims his fiery darts at those warriors who pose the greatest threat to his wicked schemes.

But before you put this book back on the shelf and decide not to learn the art of war, consider that to live in the full power and presence of God, we need to engage the battle. The problem in the world today is that we reflect God's shadow rather than God's glory. My husband, Tom, said this well Sunday morning in his sermon: "The world is not full of lost people because the devil is so strong. The world is full of lost people because the church is so weak."

My friend, the church is weak because the people who profess to know Christ as Lord are not serious about serving His cause. We would rather eat the royal food than take a stand that tells the world, "We refuse to defile our bodies with the extravagant diet you have to offer!" Daniel and his friends took a stand that landed them in a furnace and a lion's den. But their willingness to fear God more than they feared the devil opened the floodgates of heaven, and the King of Glory came in.

You might want to pause right now and decide. Do you want to win battles or would you rather sip wine and nibble on delicacies? One life will demonstrate the glory of God; the other *may* be somewhat safe—there are no guarantees. But a life lived in weak and wimpy "devotion" will most definitely NOT advance God's kingdom on earth. What will you do with your life?

FAITHFULNESS TO GOD REWARDED

Daniel, Shadrach, Meshach, and Abednego continued to live their lives faithful to God in the pagan culture of Babylon. Because Nebuchadnezzar was impressed with them, they were later placed in positions of authority (Daniel 2:46–49). When God's choice servants walked out their faith, God granted them positions of authority and power. He let His favor rest on them, and through their places of privilege they were able to influence others by their devotion to God.

However, the devil wasn't happy with this, so he tried to bring them down.

THE FIERY FURNACE

Please read Daniel 3 in your favorite translation of the Bible. I'm going to retell the story right now, and I want you to check me for accuracy.

King Nebuchadnezzar was feeling pretty good about himself and all his success, so he made a huge image of . . . himself . . . and set it out in a field. He wanted everyone to see what a great statue he'd made, so he called all his most important people together for a big celebration and dedication of his piece of art.

This included just about anybody and everybody who claimed to be somebody in the Babylonian empire. Of course Shadrach, Meshach, and Abednego were part of this group. So once everyone was gathered together out in that field where Nebuchadnezzar's statue stood, Nebuchadnezzar had his herald shout, "Everybody! When you hear the sound of the band, you must fall down and worship this golden statue that King Nebuchadnezzar has set up. If you don't fall down and worship this statue, you will immediately be thrown into a blazing furnace."

There you have it . . . fall down and worship the idol or be thrown into a fiery furnace. All the VIPs considered their options and waited for the band to play. As soon as they heard the sound, at the very first note of the tune, all the people—everyone who had gathered in that field—fell down and worshiped the king's golden image . . .

. . . all except Shadrach, Meshach, and Abednego.

The astrologers had taken it upon themselves to be field monitors that day, so when Shadrach, Meshach, and Abednego remained standing while everyone else was bowing, they went to King Nebuchadnezzar and said, "O King, live forever!" (That is always a good way to greet a pompous king.)

"You told us to bow down to your glorious, magnificent, unsurpassed golden statue when we heard the sound of the lovely band. And you said that whoever didn't fall down and worship your amazing idol would be thrown into a blazing furnace. Well, we hate to mention this right now at such a fantastic moment in your life—when everyone who is anyone is bowing down at your command—but those Jews, the ones you seem to like so much . . . well [they paused as they cleared their throats and mustered up their nerve], those three that you put in charge of the province of Babylon, you know, Shadrach, Meshach, and Abednego, well, those men . . . King Nebuchadnezzar, *those three Jews* ignored you! They refused to serve your gods and they refused to bow down to your beautiful idol!"

This made King Nebuchadnezzar furious. And if there is one thing you will learn about King Nebuchadnezzar when you read the book of Daniel, it is that he had a very bad temper. So in his rage, King Nebuchadnezzar had Shadrach, Meshach, and Abednego brought to him, and he said, "Is this true, Shadrach, Meshach, and Abednego? Do you not serve my gods? Did you refuse to bow down to my golden image? Did you misunderstand the signal? I said to bow down when you heard the sound of the band—what part of that command did you not understand? If you misunderstood my instructions, then fall down right now and it will be fine. But if you refuse to bow down, you will be thrown immediately into a blazing furnace! Then who's going to save you?"

At this part of the story I wonder if the furnace had been lit. I wonder if the smoke of it was wafting through the air. Where was this furnace? Was it the furnace used to melt the gold that built the idol? Did they light it that morning while the band was warming up and honored guests were enjoying their cheese and wine? Did it crackle and pop, providing a kind of percussion for the concert as a subtle reminder that what King Nebuchadnezzar wants King Nebuchadnezzar gets? If this was the case, then Shadrach, Meshach, and Abednego knew their confession could very well be the end of them.

I wonder if they told the king they needed to discuss their answer for a minute. I wonder if they huddled up and talked about the pros and cons of dying over such a silly thing. I mean, they could just bow down to the golden idol, get back home far away from the king, and keep doing good work for the Lord. What good would they be to God if they were dead?

Or did Shadrach, Meshach, and Abednego immediately answer their king with their solemn refusal to worship any lesser gods? Were they so committed to serving God that they didn't even have to consider their answer?

A PERSONAL UNDERSTANDING OF SHADRACH, MESHACH, AND ABEDNEGO'S RESPONSE

In the past few months I've had two opportunities to stand in Shadrach, Meshach, and Abednego's shoes. Now, we aren't under the rule of a wicked king in middle Tennessee, and no one's built an idol at the Titans' stadium and invited me to worship it. (If they had, the idol would have been submerged in flood waters back in May and we would have had to wear snorkels and masks to gather there.) But I have had two moments in time where I had to choose whom I would serve.

In the first situation I had to decide if I was going to serve the fear of cancer or if I was going to trust the love of God. I went in for a colonoscopy on March 1. I knew things were not right in me, but I'd put off having the procedure because . . . well, I don't really have a good reason for putting it off except maybe because the doctor I had to go to was a childhood friend of my husband's. He was the quarterback of the Dickson County High School football team, for heaven's sake (Go Cougars!), and I just didn't feel comfortable having to discuss my private matters with one of Tom's schoolmates.

But my symptoms grew worse, so I finally "got my guts up." (This is a great term that my daughter came up with when she went to meet her boyfriend's mother for the first time. Even now I smile as I remember her saying it to me the day I took her to their house.) I made an appointment with Dr. Max Caudill.

Colonoscopies are not terrible. In fact, I rather enjoyed mine (all except the preparation beforehand). For me the procedure consisted of a needle put in my hand, a euphoric nap, then waking to the feeling that all is as it should be in my world. Only, just before Tom and I prepared to leave, Dr. Caudill sat down beside me on my gurney, put his arm around my shoulders, and said, "Leighann, we have a problem. You have cancer."

Unless you've heard those words, you cannot begin to imagine how my world stopped spinning. The psalmist referenced a similar moment with this verse: "The cords of death entangled me, the anguish of the grave came upon me; I was overcome by trouble and sorrow" (Psalm 116:3).

For fifteen minutes I was in a free fall. Immediately I started weeping. I looked at Tom and his face reflected a serious resolve that somehow, some way we were going to get through this. After the preliminaries were discussed and Dr. Caudill left us alone, Tom said to me, "Leighann, this is not your cancer, it is ours. Every step of the way we are going to do this together."

I loved that response of my good husband. Tom didn't say, "Leighann, you're going to win this battle. You're going to live. We're going to kick the devil in the teeth. This cancer's got nothing on us! We'll be done with this in no time."

That's exactly what happened. But on March 1, all we knew was that I had a considerably large cancerous tumor in my colon, and it could have already spread to my liver and/or lungs. We didn't have a clue how serious my cancer was, and since we'd already seen wonderful, godly people die of cancer (younger than me), we didn't know what might happen next. So Tom's response was the most loving, reassuring thing he could say (and the most comforting). I would not be alone (ever) in my cancer journey. I want you to know that Tom is still fulfilling that promise he made to me.

But even with Tom's encouragement I saw my life literally fast-forward before my eyes. I saw my children's high school graduations.

Chances were I'd make it to Mikel's (hers was just two months away), but Kaleigh's a year later and TJ's two years after that might never happen for me. I saw the weddings I'd miss and the grandbabies I'd never hold. I winced at the thought that my parents might bury me and that Tom would marry someone else. Then I just hated the fact that *she* would be so much nicer to him and he'd eventually like her more. Within the first fifteen minutes of discovering I had cancer, I was already jealous of Tom's next wife.

In shock we left the doctor's office and rode the elevator to the first floor. While I remained silent, God's Spirit took authority over the thoughts, fears, and dread that threatened to consume me. By the time Tom and I got to the car, I looked at him and said, "I'm not afraid to die. I believe what I've been teaching for twenty-plus years."

For in the fifteen minutes that it took me to find firm footing from my free fall, I realized what I always thought I knew. I realized that not only do I *hope* that God takes me to heaven when I die, I *know* that He will. I can't know this for you—but I know this for me. Jesus died on the cross. I have accepted His death as my salvation, and I know, I know, I *know* that when I die I will go to heaven to live with Him forever. The issue of my eternity was settled at the cross and confirmed at the tomb. I am saved from the cords of death.

> O death, where is thy sting? O grave, where is thy victory? The sting of death is sin; and the strength of sin is the law. But thanks be to God, which giveth us the victory through our Lord Jesus Christ.
>
> 1 Corinthians 15:55–57 KJV

From that moment forward cancer had nothing on me. There were moments when I felt sorry for myself and times when I cried, but throughout my ordeal I rested in the calm assurance of my certain salvation.

When Shadrach, Meshach, and Abednego refused to bow at that silly statue, I am convinced they rested in this same calm assurance.

I cannot share the second situation right now because it is connected with my daughter, and as God is working His wonder in our lives I will honor her privacy. I am hoping that one day she will invite me to tell her story. But without sharing details, just let me say that I am convinced that when Shadrach, Meshach, and Abednego stood before King Nebuchadnezzar, they didn't have to huddle up and discuss their options. Without even thinking, they went with God.

SHADRACH, MESHACH, AND ABEDNEGO'S POWERFUL PROFESSION

> Shadrach, Meshach and Abednego replied to the king, "O Nebuchadnezzar, we do not need to defend ourselves before you in this matter. If we are thrown into the blazing furnace, the God we serve is able to save us from it, and he will rescue us from your hand, O king. But even if he does not, we want you to know, O king, that we will not serve your gods or worship the image of gold you have set up."
>
> Daniel 3:16–18

I love that response. That kind of response did not come from a moment of inspiration. It didn't originate in ambition or greed. Theirs was not an arrogant refusal birthed out of disdain for authority or lack of respect. Shadrach, Meshach, and Abednego professed their resolve to do what they had always done: serve their God. They served God when they were young boys living in Judah. They served Him when they were taken captive years ago. They served God faithfully when God's favor resulted in prosperity and positions of power—they didn't know how else to live but to serve their God. So even in the face of what should have been considered certain death, Shadrach, Meshach, and Abednego determined to serve their God.

Before I knew the extent of my cancer, these thoughts rattled in my brain:

> "I will trust the Lord!"
> "Why wouldn't I trust God?"
> "Who would I trust if I didn't trust God?"
> "I don't even know how *not* to trust God."
> "What if He doesn't come through? What if I die?"
> "I will still trust Him!"
> "Yes, though He slay me, yet will I trust Him!" (See Job 13:15.)

I didn't have as difficult a time as you might think to embrace my faith. You see, when you make a commitment to the Lord at a young age, start taking Him at His Word, serve Him faithfully, and experience life in His presence, you really don't have any other way of thinking. It's the only life I know how to live.

Now, before you tune me out, I know that I am a rare breed—fortunate and rare. I have a friend who told me, "Leighann, you are one of the few who read God's Word, believe what He says, and accept it for what it is. But some of us, me included, don't follow God that way. We read, then we wrestle, then we try to make things work our way. Finally we come around to realize that God's Word is truth." (I might have paraphrased her exact words, but this is what they meant to me when she said them.) If you are one of those people, believe me . . . God is good. He will be faithful to His Word and He will prove himself trustworthy for you. (And I smile as I write those words, for if you are one of those people, my saying this isn't any different from God saying it, and if you won't believe Him you certainly won't believe me. So . . . I guess if that is you—go ahead! Try to prove God wrong! It simply can't be done.)

When I met with my prayer partners[2] two days after my cancer diagnosis, this is what I said: "I want you to hear me say this right here and right now at the beginning of my journey through cancer. God is God and He is good no matter how this story ends. If I live, I live to the glory of God. And if I die, I die to the glory of God. I'm serious! [They started crying.] You are my voice if I'm not here to testify. I've watched some people die to the detriment of God's glory, and I refuse to be one of those. You've got to promise me that you will not allow my death to challenge anyone's faith. God has already settled the matter of death for me; He did that on the cross. Do you promise?" I made them promise!

I can kind of relate to Shadrach, Meshach, and Abednego's profession of faith, and because I've been there I have confidence you can do the same. If you have accepted Jesus as your Lord and Savior, He *will* walk with you through the fire.

Thankfully God saw fit to miraculously save me from even a serious battle with cancer. My tumor was confined to the inside of my colon and no cancer cells were found in my lymph nodes. Right now (it will be three months tomorrow since I had my surgery), I have only a 13 percent chance of having cancer invade my body again. That percentage will decrease each year. If I make it five years I will be declared *cured*. Now, won't that be a **glory to God** day!

SEVEN TIMES HOTTER

When Shadrach, Meshach, and Abednego told King Nebuchadnezzar that they would have to go with God, Nebuchadnezzar's terrible temper got the best of him again and he commanded his soldiers to fire up the furnace seven times hotter than usual. I'm not sure

A Personal Note to Those Fighting Cancer

You might not have the same cancer story. You might be facing a serious battle with cancer even now, enduring the nausea and hair loss after treatment and more than one surgery in a fight for your life. I have to tell you that I was confused and even "miffed" to have fought and won my battle so quickly. I felt guilty and didn't really know what to do with my miracle. As I talked to God about this, He simply said, "This is **your** story, this is **your** song. Tell it for my glory." And so I hope that you will find encouragement in my experience and that at the same time you will be an encouragement to others through yours. You can learn more about the battles we fight for our health in chapter 10.

how hot the furnace usually was, but I'm sure it was hot enough to burn a few Jewish men who dared to defy the king. However, King Nebuchadnezzar wanted to make a statement with these three, and so he set his fire to blazing even hotter than hot.

Then the king had Shadrach, Meshach, and Abednego tied up. In Daniel 3:21 we read that they were tied up with their clothes on—their robes, tunics, turbans, and whatever else they were wearing. King Nebuchadnezzar's soldiers took Shadrach, Meshach, and Abednego, all bound up and ready to die, and tossed them into the furnace. The furnace was so hot that it killed the soldiers who threw them in! Now think about that for a moment. Each man was most likely tossed into that furnace by two or three other men. So before they were in the fire, that fire already took the lives of perhaps nine of King Nebuchadnezzar's strongest soldiers.

Once they were in the flames, Shadrach, Meshach, and Abednego experienced the love of God like they had never experienced it before. The God they faithfully served danced with them in the flames. The furnace only burned the ropes that were used to tie Shadrach, Meshach, and Abednego up. What about that?! The very furnace that was built to destroy them instead burned away the chains that bound them! If you feel like you are in the furnace today, perhaps God is doing this same thing for you. The fire you are in is not there to destroy you but instead is built to burn through the ropes that bind you from being free to dance with the Lord!

> Then King Nebuchadnezzar leaped to his feet in amazement and asked his advisors, "Weren't there three men that we tied up and threw into the fire?"
>
> They replied, "Certainly, O king."
>
> He said, "Look, I see four men walking around in the fire, unbound and unharmed, and the fourth looks like a son of the gods."
>
> Daniel 3:24–25

Shadrach, Meshach, and Abednego determined to serve the Lord. That determination invited warfare into their lives. Their enemy created a furnace and threatened to destroy them. They resolved that if they died, they died. But either way, live or die, they were going to do so to the glory of God. So God took the furnace that was designed to destroy them and turned it into a place where they learned that they were "free to dance."

FREE TO DANCE

Yesterday when I sat down to start working on this book, I opened up the notebook I used last spring to teach my class. Inside the front pocket was a card. Women brought me cards often, and because I was busy talking, I sometimes tucked the cards in my notebook and forgot all about them. This particular card contained a letter written by my friend Sharon. She wrote it the week after my cancer surgery, but I didn't read it until yesterday. In just a minute I'm going to share with you what she wrote, but before I do I want you to know that the battle I am fighting right now for the life, future, and well-being of my daughter (and grandchild) is much larger than the skirmish I endured with cancer. It doesn't even begin to compare to the flood. Tom and I have begun to think that the cancer and the flood might have been boot camp training for war, and this is war. If you have ever known the pain of your children running opposite of God's best for their lives, you know what I am trying to put into words.

So the fact that I didn't read Sharon's letter until yesterday is just another of those supernatural kisses from the mouth of God that I consider "pure joy" in my "various trials" (James 1:2). This is what Sharon wrote:

> A few months ago I felt the urge to write you a note or send a quick e-mail just to let you know how much I appreciate you and your dedication to TSC's women's ministry. I had noticed some similarities in us (especially where our kids are concerned) and that gives me great hope as someone who admires you [Sharon doesn't know about my daughter yet]. Unfortunately I often have good intentions of writing a note but fail in the follow-through. ☺
>
> A few months later you were diagnosed with cancer. That really messed me up because now I thought, "If I send a note now she'll think it's because she has cancer." So I waited.
>
> A few weeks later you were sitting before the church with your sweet family while we had the honor of praying for you. As I was praying, I kept hearing the phrase "free to dance." I felt compelled to pray that over you and did so out loud. Okay, not LOUD but out loud. ☺ I just prayed that through it all you would be free to dance. I

even thought, "Maybe I should send her a note." But then I thought, "What if she thinks I'm nuts or that I'm just trying to get in her business?" . . .

Then . . . Julie told me about her ideas for tonight and BAM! [Julie invited children to dance as part of the worship experience the week after my surgery.] The phrase "free to dance" came full circle and hit me in the face. So . . . here is my long overdue note.

I am one of many who love and appreciate you; one of many who are inspired and challenged by you; one of many who have prayed for you and rejoiced with you during this journey. I will continue to pray and trust that as each day passes you will become more and more . . .

FREE TO DANCE!

Another one of His dancers,
Sharon

WHAT LOVE DOES

As I wrote this chapter, I didn't have a clue it would lead toward being "free to dance." I didn't orchestrate my story to lead to the letter from Sharon; that's just where God took me. When I had cancer I was ready to *fight*. I mean, I was teaching on spiritual warfare, the Enemy handed me cancer, and I was off and running. Tom and I were digging in. We fully anticipated a five- to seven-day stay at the hospital (we spent two nights there) and chemo treatments for the next six months. We were going to walk with our heads held high and our banners waving.

But God nipped my cancer in the bud. I had surgery on Tuesday and my surgeon called me Friday at home with the incredible news that of the twenty-two lymph nodes they'd taken to pathology, zero came back with cancer. We were so surprised that we didn't really know what to do. Like I said before, I felt a twinge of guilt.

For the next little while I tried to make sense of what my cancer was all about. Why did I get away so easy when others had to fight for their lives?

Then the flood came and destroyed our worship center and children's classrooms. That too happened fast, and our heads were spinning. But we had volunteers respond so quickly and generously that we never ever gave the Enemy credit for that one. Then our church collected an offering of over $230,000 in one Sunday service a few weeks ago, and that was more than enough to pay for the damage (because of the generosity of volunteers, the estimated cost was right at $200,000). Today our church is giving the extra money we collected to others in middle Tennessee who are still rebuilding from their flood damage. God just shut the devil up with the flood.

But now Tom and I are fighting a battle we never dreamed we'd be fighting. Thus far it just seems to be getting worse. But because God brought us through the cancer, and because He brought us through the flood, we are confident He will keep His promises regarding our daughter.

I don't know what kind of boot camp training God is allowing in your life. I don't know what kind of battles you might be fighting, but Sharon's note reminds us that in the midst of the fire we are *free to dance*. My friend, that's what God's love does.

What Love Does

Have you ever danced in the fire? How did it feel?

Read Daniel 3:26–30. As a result of their devotion to God, Shadrach, Meshach, and Abednego were promoted to even higher positions of honor in the pagan empire of Babylon. And God was glorified.

How might God bring glory to himself in the battles you face today?

Begin your prayer with this:

Father, I'm amazed at what your love does. When I face the "various trials" that come my way, teach me to recognize the "pure joy" that you supply with them (James 1:2). When the devil attacks my life, remind me that attack comes with an invitation to experience what your love does. Help me to grow so in my faith that like Shadrach, Meshach, and Abednego, I can choose to serve only you. I love you, Lord. I trust you, and I'm going to keep reading this book because I want my life to bring glory to your name.

SHARPEN YOUR SWORD

God's love for you will never be removed. Isaiah 54:10

All things work together for good. Romans 8:28

Every attack from the Enemy brings with it an invitation to experience the love of God. Philippians 3:10

Nothing can separate you from the love of God. Romans 8:38–39

Commit the Word to memory: The next time you take a shower, sing a verse to a familiar tune. "Three Blind Mice" and "Old McDonald" are good tunes to try. Make a joyful noise and sharpen your sword!

Chapter Three

Love's Completed Work

> For I am the least of the apostles, unworthy to be called an apostle, because I persecuted the church of God. But by God's grace I am what I am, and His grace toward me was not ineffective. However, I worked more than any of them, yet not I, but God's grace that was with me.
>
> 1 Corinthians 15:9–10 HCSB

GOD IS LOVE

We've discussed God's love and what God's love does. In this chapter we are going to embrace love's completed work. If God is love, let's call God **Love**. First John 4:8 states this truth: "Whoever does not love does not know God, because God is *love*."

First John 3:16 tells us how we know what love is: "This is how we know what love is: Jesus Christ laid down his life for us."

Love completed His work on the cross. See how that is demonstrated when we simply insert **Love** in the place of God in the following verses:

"For **Love** did not send His Son into the world to condemn the world, but to save the world through him."

John 3:17

"**Love** did not spare his own Son, but gave him up for us all—how will he not also, along with him, graciously give us all things?"

Romans 8:32

THE POWER OF THE CROSS

I didn't serve in leadership among women for long before I decided that leading women was like trying to herd cats. Women are not easily led. There are many reasons we aren't good followers, but one reason rises above the others when it comes to serving God and His church.

We feel inadequate. We are insecure, and we live defeated lives. These inner battles tend to make us a bit prickly on the outside. We *know* that Jesus died on the cross to save us from our sins, but somewhere along the way saving us from our sins was something He did way back when. Even though we don't want to admit it, we kind of think His death was only sufficient enough to save us from "most of our sins." We don't understand the power of the cross.

Let me see if I can explain this to you. Several years ago Tom and I traveled to Fort Lauderdale to attend an Evangelism Explosion training event. EE has now been updated and is called Everyday Evangelism. It is a proven, effective way to train believers in embracing a lifestyle of witnessing. Our evangelism pastor wanted Tom and me to really buy in to this method of evangelism training, so he enrolled us in the clinic that would be taught by Dr. D. James Kennedy, EE's founder and the pastor of Coral Ridge Presbyterian Church. In the course of his ministry Dr. Kennedy counseled presidents and was well respected as a major influence on national politics. In addition to his promotion of conservative Christian values in the political arena, he created the EE plan for teaching and training people to share their faith. Dr. Kennedy was famous. Tom and I were eager to meet him.

On the second day of our EE clinic, the trainer told us that two of us would have the privilege of making our visit (something they call "on the job training") with Dr. Kennedy. Each night of the clinic we divided into teams of two clinicians and one trained mentor, and the three of us went out to share our faith with strangers. Some of the teams went to visit people who'd attended Sunday's services at Coral Ridge, and others went to meet people outside Laundromats or grocery stores. When the trainer told us that two of us would get to take our visit with Dr. Kennedy, I hoped that Tom would be one of the two chosen, at the same time hoping that I would NOT. Tom is not intimidated by famous people—I am. After our break, the announcement was made and guess who got the privilege of making an EE visit with Dr. Kennedy—me.

The time for our visit came. My new friend, a seminary student from Miami, and I met Dr. Kennedy in his office. It was then that I discovered that Dr. Kennedy's visits came to him—he didn't go to them. As Dr. Kennedy welcomed us I couldn't help but notice the pictures hanging on the walls. They were of Dr. Kennedy shaking hands with every U.S. president who'd held office in the past forty years. I wondered at the places God has taken me in my adventure with Him. Here I was in Dr. D. James Kennedy's office with a seminary student from Miami participating in small talk.

Mr. Sanders (fictional name) arrived for his appointment with Dr. Kennedy on time and we were all introduced. Dr. Kennedy asked me to explain to Mr. Sanders the grace of God. I can't remember a word I said, but my explanation led Dr. Kennedy into a thorough discussion of a grace vs. works theology. He chose Ephesians 2:8–10 as the basis of his teaching:

> For it is by grace you have been saved, through faith—and this is not from yourselves, it is a gift of God—not by works, so that no one can boast. For we are God's workmanship, created in Christ Jesus to do good works, which God prepared in advance for us to do.

I listened as Dr. Kennedy explained that we cannot add anything to, nor can we take anything away from the gift of God, which was the sacrificial, substitute death of His "one and only Son" that day on the cross. He explained that when Jesus died for us He accomplished our salvation all by himself. Salvation is not earned; it can only be received.

Through the years I've heard Dr. Kennedy's voice echo in my ears. The same voice that counseled presidents spoke this powerful truth to me. Jesus Christ died so that we might live. When Jesus died on the cross, He broke the chains of sin and set the captives free. Titus 3 sums up what I heard Dr. Kennedy explain that night in his office.

> For we too were once foolish, disobedient, deceived, captives of various passions and pleasures, living in malice and envy, hateful, detesting one another. But when the goodness and love for man appeared from God our Savior, He saved us—not by works of righteousness that we had done, but according to His mercy, through the washing of regeneration and renewal by the Holy Spirit. This [Spirit] He poured out on us abundantly through Jesus Christ our Savior, so that having been justified by His grace, we may become heirs with the hope of eternal life. This saying is trustworthy. I want you to insist on these things, so that those who have believed God might be careful to devote themselves to good works. These are good and profitable for everyone.
>
> Titus 3:3–8 HCSB

We do good works because we have been saved by God's amazing grace—not because we hope to gain or merit His favor. God freely poured His grace on us simply because He loves us. "But God demonstrates his own love for us in this: While we were yet sinners, Christ died for us" (Romans 5:8).

To quote my husband again, "The only thing I bring to my salvation is the sin that nailed Jesus to the cross."

THE PASSION OF THE CHRIST

I'm sure you've either seen or heard of *The Passion of the Christ*, a gruesomely vivid portrayal of Jesus' sacrificial death. I went to see *The Passion* when it came out in the theaters. I could tell you I saw it, but that would be an exaggeration. I sat in the room where it was showing and covered my eyes with the palms of my hands so that I could plug my ears with my fingers. I did peek out a few times and saw parts of the movie.

Each year on Good Friday we show a scaled-back version of *The Passion of the Christ* as part of a prayer labyrinth we set up at our church. We invite people to reflect on the "passion" of Christ. It was only a few years ago when I finally understood the term *the passion of the Christ*. When Jesus met the soldiers who came for Him in the garden, He set His face to the cross and never looked back. It is one thing for a man to do that if he has no choice, but quite another for a man to choose to take that journey. Jesus chose the cross. He was compelled by love.

Jesus' *passion* for us forced Him to embrace the cross. The origin of our word *passion* comes from the Greek word *paschō*, which means "to suffer." But you're probably more familiar with the more common meaning of passion: fervent love. Understanding both meanings helped me understand *the passion of the Christ*. Because Jesus was consumed with love for us, He embraced the suffering of the cross.

Let's take a selah moment. (*Selah* means a dramatic pause for contemplation and reflection.) Jesus' love for you kept Him from calling ten thousand angels to come to His rescue. Jesus' love for you kept His head bowed low when the Roman soldiers stripped the flesh from His back. Jesus' love for you held Him to the cross.

I'm not sure we take nearly enough time to linger at that old rugged cross.

I grew up in a hymn-singing church. When I am in the midst of battle (like I am today), it is the hymns that come to my mind. Two nights ago Tom and I sat on our porch swing and sang every old hymn we could remember. It was not very pretty (we are not singers), more of the joyful noise kind of singing, but we were both encouraged and I am certain God smiled. One old hymn that I used to sing to my babies when I rocked them in the night was this:

> On a hill far away, stood an old rugged cross,
> the emblem of suffering and shame.
> And I love that old cross where the dearest and best
> for a world of lost sinners was slain.
> So I'll cherish the old rugged cross,
> till my trophies at last I lay down.
> I will cling to the old rugged cross,
> and exchange it someday for a crown.[1]

EMBRACING THE OLD RUGGED CROSS

We need to learn to truly embrace that old rugged cross. When I travel and teach on spiritual warfare, I'm consistently faced with stories of women who are convinced that *they* have out-sinned God's grace. They don't serve Jesus with the gifts He's given them to serve Him. They don't live the victorious lives He's offered them. Instead they live their difficult lives under the oppressive lies of the devil because they *think* they've gone too far, done too much, waited too long, and out-sinned the love of God.

Two truths I want to shout aloud to combat this wicked lie are these:

1. **It's never too late to start doing what's right.**
2. **As long as you are in the land of the living there is hope.**

You cannot out-sin the love of God. You can't, it's impossible! I don't care if you slept with your husband's best friend, told Ethel Mabel's deepest darkest secret, ate the last cookie in the cookie jar and blamed it on your son, or ran off to Vegas and became a showgirl.

You cannot do *anything* to take away from Jesus' death on the cross.

Too many times we teach on the other side of this truth. We proclaim boldly that there is nothing we can add to our salvation, but we don't explain the powerful truth that neither can we subtract from it. For instance, you cannot be saved by grace but then live by works. The same grace that saved you is the grace that sustains you. You don't "do good works" to impress God. You don't serve the church or feed the poor to get God to answer your prayers better. He just loves you—that's it. He loves you so completely that He can't love you more. You do good works because you're amazed by His grace.

I understood this truth so well on the night I faced my daughter in her mess. I am trying hard not to go into too much detail for her sake, but Mikel stood on the sidewalk in front of her apartment with her arms crossed and her jaw set (she got the jaw-set thing from her dad, not me), and she dared us to take her home. She'd made up her mind, and nothing we could say or do was going to change it. She broke my heart that night, but I have never loved her more . . . not when she scored the game-winning run, not when she made straight A's (which she did often including this last semester of high school). I have never loved my daughter more than when she defied me that night. You see, Mikel cannot do *anything* that will make me love her more and she cannot do *anything* that will make me love her less. I *love* Mikel, Kaleigh, and TJ. I love each of them with all I have. I think this is what God meant when He said that He loved us like a mother.

> Can a mother forget the baby at her breast and have no compassion on the child she has borne? Though she may forget, I will not forget you! See, I have engraved you on the palms of my hands; your walls are ever before me.
>
> Isaiah 49:15–16

I "get" this verse because I nursed my children. And I know, from experience, that it would be impossible for a mother to forget her nursing child. Even if she were so scatterbrained that she simply "forgot" she had a baby, or if she were so unkind that she "chose" to forget him, she couldn't physically do it. For when that baby didn't drink that milk, her perfect "to go" containers—the ones God gave her to feed her child—would remind her she had a baby to feed. But God went one step further when He gave this word to Isaiah. He said, "Even *if* she were to forget, I will *not* forget you." Think about that for another selah moment.

IS IT FINISHED?

Back to the women I know and love. When our mistakes create messes, we tend to beat ourselves to a pulp. Believe you me, I've been there and I fight this daily. How many nights have I lain awake and played the game called "What Was I Thinking?!" How many moments do I wish I could erase? How may do-overs do I wish I could take? Plenty!

But it occurred to me one day that when I keep myself stirred up over the mistakes I've made, I'm in essence saying, "Jesus, you didn't do enough." You see, if my mistakes and failures have somehow done irreversible damage to me (or the people I love) and rendered me useless to the kingdom of God, then Jesus didn't complete His work on the cross that day.

The apostle Paul had this thought a long time before I did. Paul admitted that he didn't "even deserve to be called an apostle" (1 Corinthians 15:9). Let's stop here. Do you ever feel like you don't deserve to be used by God? Does the Enemy tell you that you are no longer worthy to be called His precious daughter? Do you ever think you have nothing to offer because . . .

. . . you got pregnant when you were a teen, had an abortion, committed adultery, divorced your husband, lied, cheated, or got yourself addicted to prescription drugs? Do you sit on the sidelines of kingdom work because you are overweight or uneducated or because you failed the last time you tried? These are the LIES I'm talking about! Either Jesus completed the work of salvation by enduring the shame and suffering of the cross or He didn't. It can't be both ways.

When Jesus declared the work of salvation complete, it was *finished*!

Who would know better the degree of suffering required to satisfy the wrath of God than His very own Son? When you or I hang our heads and shuffle our feet, when we allow the Enemy to whisper lies in our ears—lies that stop us from fulfilling the *good work* God prepared beforehand for us to do—we are in essence standing at the foot of the cross, wagging our fingers in the face of our dying Savior, and shouting, "You didn't suffer enough!"

Do you want to do that?! Go watch *The Passion of the Christ* without covering your eyes and without plugging your ears, then tell me He didn't do enough for you.

I know this is difficult truth I am sharing with you. And believe you me, if I weren't so angry at the Enemy for holding countless women captive with this very lie, I wouldn't be so blunt. But it's time for us to crucify this lie on the cross where Jesus died.

Jesus' final words were true. "It *is* finished."

Only Christ knew when it was done. Only He knew how bad sin hurt. Only Jesus knew how long He had to suffer. When He paid for our sins He paid for them all. The ones we committed before we knew Him and the ones we'll commit from this day until the day we go to live with Him forever in heaven. Jesus died for them all. He died for the ones that you dismiss and He died for the ones that haunt you. Jesus died for them all.

> Jesus paid it all,
> All to Him I owe.
> Sin had left a crimson stain;
> He washed me white as snow.[2]

Paul knew this truth.

> For I am the least of the apostles and do not even deserve to be called an apostle, because I persecuted the church of God. *But by the grace of God I am what I am, and his grace to me was not without effect.*
>
> 1 Corinthians 15:9–10

Don't you love that part? "But by the grace of God I am what I am, and his grace to me was not without effect." If you can say that with Paul, say it aloud! Shout it from the rooftops and declare it in the streets.

BY THE GRACE OF GOD I AM WHAT I AM!

I humbly bow at the foot of the cross because that is where my Savior died. Would you bow there with me? Will you lay down the sin that the Enemy holds over you? That sin's power is broken, the chains are gone.

> This righteousness from God comes through faith in Jesus Christ to all who believe. There is no difference, for all have sinned and fall short of the glory of God [those who sinned much and those who sinned little], and are justified freely by his grace through

> the redemption that came by Christ Jesus. God presented him as a sacrifice of atonement, through faith in his blood.
>
> ROMANS 3:22–25

> You have been set free from sin and have become slaves to righteousness.
>
> ROMANS 6:18

There is one more part of Paul's declaration in 1 Corinthians 15 that I want you to understand.

> For I am the least of the apostles and do not even deserve to be called an apostle, because I persecuted the church of God. But by the grace of God I am what I am, and his grace to me was not without effect. *No, I worked harder than all of them—yet not I, but the grace of God that was with me*.
>
> 1 CORINTHIANS 15:9–10

Did you get the last part? Once Paul declared himself "unworthy," he reminded himself of the grace of God. Then, he determined that God's grace would not stop with merely paying for his sin. The grace that saved Paul would be the same grace that worked in and through Paul to accomplish good works. And just look at the good works that Paul accomplished! When you decide to allow God's grace to completely erase your sin, you are free to allow His grace to work through you to fulfill the many plans God has for your life. Until then you need to remain at the foot of the cross.

AMAZING GRACE

I love the fact that God planted churches, fueled the Christian movement, and wrote most of the New Testament through a sinner/saint like Paul. I love it because I can identify with him. Paul's story tells me that even when I mess up, and even if I mess up royally, God's grace is enough.

I cannot tell you how many ways I paved my daughter's path right out of God's best for her life. I'm not taking personal responsibility for her free will (even she made sure we knew that she was choosing this herself), but I do see many ways that I was duped by the devil. I'm wrestling with that right now. But as I've written these truths, I'm convinced that when God made me a mother, He took into account the mistakes I would make. I'm not sure that He answered my prayers for children because He thought I'd do such a good job. Instead, I'm inclined to believe that He banked on His very own *grace* to cover all my mistakes.

God has done that in my marriage, He's done that in the ministry where I have served Him, He's done that in my friendships, and He will do that in the lives of my children. The best part of this: He's good at it! God is good at transforming our messes into miracles. He gets lots of practice daily. What would I do without His amazing grace? Where would I be today? How would I lay my head down at night and open my eyes tomorrow if I didn't believe God's grace was enough?

> But he said to me, "My grace is sufficient for you, for my power is made perfect in weakness." Therefore I will boast all the more gladly about my weaknesses, so that Christ's power may rest on me.
>
> 2 Corinthians 12:19

I was attending a church service on a Bahamian island when an inebriated man took a seat in the pew in front of me. It was a small island, a place where everyone knew everyone and where everyone went to church. The island was "dry," with no alcohol served or sold in any restaurant or store. But somehow this man, known as the island drunk, found the liquid that held him captive. When he stumbled down the church aisle, he commandeered stares from the little girls who sat on the pew to his right. Their eyes darted from him to their mothers, seeming to say, "I can't believe he's here!"

I watched as he spoke loudly to the family sitting next to him and wondered if he'd be a distraction in the service. But he maintained some dignity and listened respectfully to the various speakers and singers. When we worshiped, he sang loud with great emotion, and during one chorus I saw him weep uncontrollably. I was somewhat impressed that even in his inebriated condition, his was a picture of humility before the Lord.

We were singing the very last song at the end of the service when he did what I was afraid he'd do the whole night—he spoke out loud, shouting from his pew on the fifth row to my friend who was leading worship on the platform.

"Can we sing it one more time for me, buddy, just one more time for me?"

> Amazing grace, how sweet the sound,
> That saved a wretch like me.
> I once was lost but now am found,
> Was blind but now I see.
>
> 'Twas grace that taught my heart to fear.
> And grace my fears relieved.
> How precious did that grace appear
> The hour I first believed.[3]

How long has it been since you wept over all your sin? How long has it been since you experienced grace and were baffled by how amazing God's grace truly is? In the madness of life, we pack our days full of so much that we seldom take time to ponder those things that ought to amaze us.

Things like . . . grace.

Grace that saved a wretch like me—

Grace that made my eyes to see—
Grace that taught my heart to fear—
And grace my fears relieved—

> Through many dangers, toils and snares
> I have already come;
> 'Tis grace hath brought me safe thus far,
> And grace will lead me home.
>
> When we've been there ten thousand years,
> Bright shining as the sun,
> We've no less days to sing God's praise
> Than when we'd first begun.[4]

And perhaps you've never heard this nearly forgotten verse that Newton added near the end of his song:

> The earth shall soon dissolve like snow,
> The sun forbear to shine;
> But God, who called me here below,
> Will be forever mine.

Love's Completed Work

Read Romans 6:23.

Thank God that you don't have to receive the wages you earned.

. . . for the wages of sin is ____________.

Thank Him for His free gift of eternal life.

. . . but the ____________ of God is ____________ life.

Give God whatever it is that Satan convinced you He didn't want. Give Him the lie that disqualified you from living the life Jesus died for you to live. Then sing this song for your prayer today:

Amazing grace, how sweet the sound,
That saved a wretch like me.
I once was lost but now am found,
Was blind but now I see.

'Twas grace that taught my heart to fear,
And grace my fears relieved.
How precious did that grace appear
The hour I first believed.

Through many dangers, toils and snares
I have already come;
'Twas grace that brought me safe thus far,
And grace will lead me home.

When we've been there ten thousand years,
Bright shining as the sun,
We've no less days to sing God's praise
Than when we'd first begun.

The earth shall soon dissolve like snow,
The sun forbear to shine;
But God, who called me here below,
Will be forever mine.[5]

SHARPEN YOUR SWORD

God is love. 1 John 4:8

God demonstrated His love for us on the cross. John 3:16–17; Romans 5:8; 8:32

Jesus' death completed God's labor of love. John 19:30

God's grace is enough. 2 Corinthians 12:9

Commit the Word to memory: Enlist a memory partner and play games with your verses. One of you start quoting and let the other finish. This is a great game to play with family members.

PART TWO

THE ENEMY EXPOSED

In any warfare waged by the enemy against the individual believer, the primary battlefield is the *mind.* The goal of our warfare as stated in 2 Corinthians 10:5 is to steal back our thought life and take it captive to Christ instead. The enemy's chief target is the mind because the most effective way to influence behavior is to influence thinking. Our minds are the control centers of our entire beings. The enemy knows far better than we do that nothing is bigger or more powerful than God. That's why everything that "exalts itself" in our thought life is called a "pretension." Satan plays make-believe. He can only pretend because he lost all rights to presume authority over the believer's life when Christ, "having disarmed the powers and authorities, . . . made a public spectacle of them, triumphing over them by the cross" (Col. 2:15). Unfortunately, Satan is very good at his job because he's had so much experience. He plays make-believe and does a remarkable job of trying to make us believe it. Repeat after me: *nothing is bigger or more powerful than God!* Absolutely nothing![1]

Beth Moore, *Praying God's Word*

Chapter Four

Spiritual Warfare Is Real

> Beloved, do not be surprised at the fiery ordeal among you, which comes upon you for your testing, as though some strange thing were happening to you.
>
> 1 Peter 4:12 NASB

The Bible is full of illustrations of men and women who battled the Enemy well. Scripture also contains several stories of those who were overcome by Satan's evil schemes. The reality of spiritual warfare is evident in Scripture from the beginning (in Genesis 3 when the serpent first appeared to Eve) to the end (in Revelation 20 when Satan's destiny is complete).

In the Old Testament, Israel's kings were enticed and distracted by pagan gods, described in the New Testament as "spiritual forces of evil" (see Ephesians 6:12).

Saul sought the advice of sorcerers, and Ahaz sacrificed his son in the fire of Molech. Satan requested permission to go after Job, and Daniel was subjected to the torment of Nebuchadnezzar, a king powerfully influenced by his own pagan gods in Babylon.

In the New Testament, Jesus was tempted by Satan after His forty-day fast. Permission was granted to Satan to "sift" Peter. Demons tormented children, and the apostle Paul urged believers to gear up for battle by clothing themselves in the armor of God.

Spiritual warfare is real.

Chuck Lawless, dean at Southern Seminary, has this to say about the reality of spiritual warfare:

> Both Peter and Paul knew the ferocity of the Enemy's attacks. Hence it is a little wonder that they called believers to be ever alert:
>
> - "Be sober; be vigilant, because your adversary the devil walks about like a roaring lion, seeking whom he may devour." (1 Peter 5:8)
> - "With all prayer and supplication, in the Spirit, being watchful to this end with all perseverance and supplication for all the saints." (Ephesians 6:18)
>
> Their words are strong and pointed, as both apostles understood that *all believers* are targets of the enemy. No follower of God is immune from the attacks of the one who will devour whom he can. If the enemy was brazen enough to attack Peter, Paul and *Jesus Himself* (Mt. 4:11), surely we should not expect anything less. The battle is on, whether we like it or not.[1]

And E. M. Bounds says this:

> It cannot be said too often that the life of a Christian is warfare, an intense conflict, a lifelong contest. It is a battle fought against invisible foes who are ever alert and seeking to entrap, deceive, and ruin the souls of men. . . . The Christian warrior is compelled from the hour he first draws his sword to "*endure hardness, as a good soldier*" (2 Tim. 2:3).[2]

But somehow we miss the truth of battlefield living, don't we? During my years in the ministry I've had the privilege of participating in think tanks with women's ministry resource developers. I've often been frustrated by the focus of our discussions. Most often we venture toward what women need. And that discussion leads us to begin to assess the damage the Enemy does in the lives of women, but we never talk about the *Enemy*. Women *need* to know how to have good marriages. Women *need* help parenting their children. Women *need* to overcome depression, fear, anxiety, poor self-esteem . . . the list goes on and on.

After many years of developing, writing, teaching, and selling these great products, we still find that women need something more! Could it be that we are focusing our attention in the wrong direction? Perhaps rather than helping her create a spa or coffee house on the corner of the battlefield we are careful not to mention, we ought to train women for war.

Spiritual warfare is real.

WHAT IS SPIRITUAL WARFARE?

Spiritual warfare is the ongoing struggle between God and Satan. But don't for one minute think that it is a desperate struggle between two equal but opposing forces.

Unlike God, who is Creator of the universe, Satan is a created being. And unlike God, who is head over all authority, power, dominion, and title that can be given (Ephesians 1:20–23), Satan has jurisdiction only over the earth. Satan is not equal to God in power, in rule, or in authority. He is subject to God, and his destiny is already determined. Isaiah 54:16–17 points to this truth:

> "See, it is I who created the blacksmith who fans the coals into flame and forges a weapon fit for its work. And it is I who have created the destroyer to work havoc; no weapon forged against you will prevail, and you will refute every tongue that accuses you. This is the heritage of the servants of the Lord, and this is their vindication from me," declares the Lord.

The war began in the garden of Eden when the serpent (Satan) convinced Eve to eat the fruit off the forbidden tree. We discussed this first battle thoroughly in chapter 1 and will revisit it again in chapter 5. The war began in the garden and it ended when Jesus died on the cross. Don't miss this important truth. The war ended at the cross. Jesus' death restored what Adam's sin destroyed.

> Here it is in a nutshell: Just as one person did it wrong and got us in all this trouble with sin and death, another person did it right and got us out of it. But more than just getting us out of trouble, he got us into life! One man said no to God and put many people in the wrong; one man said yes to God and put many in the right.
>
> ROMANS 5:18–19 THE MESSAGE

The prince of this world was defeated once and for all when Jesus reconciled men to himself through the perfect sacrifice of His perfect life. We discussed this amazing and powerful truth in chapter 3 and will revisit it often throughout the rest of this book.

WHY DO WE FIGHT TODAY?

So, you might ask, if the Enemy is defeated, why are we still fighting the good fight today? The battle continues today because the Prince of Darkness remains in charge of our sin-stained world (see Ephesians 2:1–2).

Satan expects to rule and reign over the mess he ordained until Jesus returns and God puts it all to rest. When Adam and Eve yielded to the temptation of Satan, they took the world God gave them—a perfect dwelling place declared "very good" by God, full of good pleasure, tasty delight, and pure joy—and they handed it over to Satan. The deceiver stole creation from the Creator. This world today is only a shadow of what would have been. It's a distorted, sin-stained shadow at that.

When you accepted Jesus as your Savior and Lord, you were targeted for attack. With that declaration of allegiance to the King of Kings and Lord of Lords, you gave up your allegiance to the prince of this world. You broke ties with the Prince of Darkness. Therefore you no longer belong to this world, and the world hates you as a result. Jesus explained it like this:

> If you belonged to the world, it would love you as its own. As it is, you do not belong to the world, but I have chosen you out of the world. That is why the world hates you.
>
> John 15:19

And then Jesus prayed for us,

> My prayer is not that you take them out of the world but that you protect them from the evil one. They are not of the world, even as I am not of it.
>
> John 17:15–16

We fight spiritual warfare today because we dare to live in the strength and power and faithful promises of God. We fight because we take God at His Word and invite Him to penetrate our darkness with His glorious light.

TO PROCLAIM OR PROFANE THE NAME OF THE LORD

Spiritual warfare has at its core the purpose of God opposed to the purposes of Satan. When people struggle to know the will of God, they have turned a deaf ear to His voice. God spoke His will clearly in the great commission (Matthew 28:18–20). God's passion is to partner with His people in dynamic intimacy and out of that partnership to make His name known among the nations. Jesus told us this just before He returned to His throne in heaven.

Satan's purpose and passion is to profane the name of the Lord. He has at the core of his being the desire to destroy God's reputation and shed doubt on His motives. Just as he did in the beginning, Satan works his way into the hearts and minds of God's children. For when he can steal the testimony of a disciple, when he can kill the joy in her heart, and when he destroys her spirit, Satan profanes the name of the Lord.

Because you are a child of the King, you are a target for attack. Every day you make decisions that will either proclaim the name of the Lord or profane the name of the Lord. There's no middle ground on this battlefield. You are either with God or you're against Him.

THE ADVANTAGES OF WARFARE TRAINING

One of my daughters dated a boy who considered joining the marines. I'm not going to share how I felt about that. But I am going to share what I learned about joining the marines. When a young person decides to commit four (or more) years of his life to the marines, he goes through an intense interview process. His parents are interviewed, his significant other (if there is one) is interviewed, he is encouraged to watch the intensity of boot camp via the Internet, and finally he undergoes a thorough physical exam. Afterward, he makes a commitment to join the marines and prepares for boot camp. This process can take months, and during those months the marine recruiting officer invites the potential candidate to join him weekly for workouts. The marines are so serious about their training for battle that they train even their potential candidates! Marine recruits are trained before they ever arrive on base for boot camp. I find that interesting.

Unlike the marines, we followers of Christ kind of wake up one day and find ourselves smack dab in the middle of a war we know nothing about. Our only training was a "sinner's prayer" and a "believer's baptism." They handed us *The Book* and off we went to fend for ourselves.

Imagine if a new recruit was treated that way by the marines. Imagine he woke up one morning and decided to join the marines. The recruiting officer welcomed him with open arms, dressed him in camo, put a "how to fight" manual in his hands, patted him on the rear, and sent him on his way to war. That's crazy!

But that's just what we do with one another. The Christian soldiers who fought before us learned a thing or two. The ones who walked with Jesus got the benefit of being taught by the Master. Even those who share space on the field with us have experienced things we could benefit from hearing. Isn't it time to learn from them? Don't you want to be prepared for this war?

For far too long we have bumbled our way about, aimless and pathetically ineffective. We spend most of our energy nursing the wounded and the rest of our energy trying to hide so we can avoid any attack at all cost. What might happen if we began to assemble our troops? What might happen if we learned how to use our weapons? What damage might we do if we quit trying to avoid the devil and actually tried to find him? What might happen if women of God were equipped for battle?

Keep reading this book and find out.

A PEEK INTO THE SPIRITUAL REALM

The book of Job gives us a peek into the spiritual realm. Job 1:1–5 introduces us to Job, a "blameless and upright" man who "feared God and shunned evil." Then verses 6–12 provide insight into what goes on in the presence of God. As the angels presented themselves to God, Satan joined them. God asked him, "Where have you come from?" And Satan answered, "From roaming through the earth and going back and forth in it." Of course that is where Satan came from; the earth is his own domain, his dwelling place.

In the following verses God bragged on Job (verse 8) and Satan challenged Job's commitment to God (verses 9–11), saying that Job's devotion was easy since God protected him from Satan's attack. And then, in verse 12, unbeknownst to faithful, "blameless and upright" Job, God agreed to put Job's faith and devotion to the test. God lifted His hedge of protection from Job and let Satan have at him. At first God refused to allow Satan to harm Job himself, but after Job successfully won that first battle with the Enemy, God even allowed Satan to afflict Job physically (see Job 2:1–7).

I don't know about you, but I'm not sure I really want to know what goes on in the spiritual realm all the time. Just imagine if you captured God's attention, He bragged on you, and then Satan asked to see what you're really made of. No, I don't envy Job, not for one second. Nor do I relate well to him. I can relate much better to Job's wife, who responded to all this attack with this statement, "Are you still holding on to your integrity? Curse God and die!" (Job 2:9). I say that with a smile on my face. While I can feel Mrs. Job's pain, I have actually never said those words—and I don't ever intend to.

However, the book of Job demonstrates the reality of spiritual warfare in full and living color. It's not a pretty picture. But throughout the entire ordeal, Job grew in his experiential knowledge of God. God's presence sustained him, and God's faithfulness won in the end.

Spiritual Warfare Is Real

Read Job 1 and 2. How did Job respond to Satan's attack? How might you have responded?

Read Job 42:2. How did Satan's attack interrupt God's plans for Job? How do the perceptions and faith of others cloud your understanding of God?

I love the fact that God's plans cannot be "thwarted." No matter what battles are raging in your life today, recognize the fact that God is sovereign. His faithfulness will come through for you.

Begin your prayer with this:

Lord, I confess that sometimes I fret over the way the battles rage against me. I worry when I ought to rejoice, and I give in to despair when I should exercise faith. Forgive me for failing to trust you. I choose to believe that you will fulfill your purpose for me. Therefore I cry out to you.

SHARPEN YOUR SWORD

Spiritual warfare is real. 1 Peter 4:12

The devil is weaker than God in both power and authority. Isaiah 54:16–17

The war was won at the cross. Romans 5:17

The battle continues because Satan still reigns over the sin-stained world today. Ephesians 2:1–2

The world hates you. John 15:19

Your victory is secure. 2 Corinthians 9:8

Commit the Word to memory: Remember when teachers made their students write things over and over for punishment? This is a great way to memorize God's Word. Choose a verse and print it ten times a day for a week. Consider printing it on sticky notes so that you can place the Word wherever you go.

Chapter Five

Who My Enemy Is

> Shining morning star, how you have fallen from the heavens! You destroyer of nations, you have been put down to the ground. You said to yourself: "I will ascend to the heavens; I will set up my throne above the stars of God. I will sit on the mount of the [gods'] assembly, in the remotest parts of the North. I will ascend above the highest clouds; I will make myself like the Most High." But you will be brought down to Sheol into the deepest regions of the Pit.
>
> Isaiah 14:12–15 HCSB

I can't remember how old I was when I discovered C. S. Lewis, but while a student at Samford University, I wrote an English Lit paper on his book *The Screwtape Letters*. That book is my inspiration for the following attempt to shed light on spiritual warfare with a feminine twist. Jezebel is a modern day Wormwood, and the following is her report to her superior, Delilah Screwtape. (In C. S. Lewis's book, Screwtape was the demon mentor and uncle of Wormwood, an eager demon apprentice.)

Dear Delilah,

The woman is almost putty in my hands. I'm amazed at how easily I can influence her. All I had to do was distract her husband last night after dinner and she assumed he was mad. Oh, the fun that followed that "misunderstanding." They shouted and said things like, "You never!" and "You're always!" and "I should've known better!" They were so worked up that by bedtime she put on the old T-shirt thing that he can't stand, crawled into bed, turned her back to him, and read that Harlequin romance she "ought not to be reading" and fell asleep. He watched the baseball game and turned the television off around midnight. It's so fun messing with their marriage.

Then, at lunch today she ordered the chicken salad sandwich, the ones they serve on the calorie-laden croissants. She loves those things, and her taste buds were just about shouting out loud when she noticed that her skinny friend Millicent ordered a tiny little fruit salad. While they talked about their Bible study (I hate those!), all the woman could think about was Millicent's 120 pounds (soaking wet). I offered visions of Millicent running on the beach wearing a modest bikini and just suggested that perhaps she might follow behind huffing and puffing in her new size-18-plus one-piece—complete with one of those sweet little skirts that are supposed to camouflage their thighs. I had her so upset over the thought of Millicent in that cute little two-piece that she snapped at her for nothing. Of course, Millicent was greatly offended even though she assured the woman that she wasn't, and as soon as Millicent said good-bye she phoned Darlene on the way home and told her all about it. Now Millicent, Darlene, and Heather (whom Darlene called just to ask Heather to "pray" for Millicent and the woman) are all mad at the woman.

And to top it all off, I brought her daughter Meagan home angry. Meagan's friend Allison told her friend Andrea that Meagan was flirting with Dalton, the boy they are all gaga over. He wants only one thing and I'm working extra hard to make sure he gets it from Meagan. That will get the woman for sure! Anyway, Meagan was hurt, and she wanted to talk to the woman about it, only the woman was so frustrated over her lunch with Millicent that she couldn't pay full attention. Meagan stormed out of the kitchen and up to her bedroom; she slammed the door behind her shouting, "You NEVER listen to me!"

The woman just put her head in her hands and wondered why she even went to Bible study this morning. Then she tossed her Bible along with her Bible study notebook on the kitchen table and went to the freezer to serve herself a big bowl of Moose Tracks ice cream.

I'd say all in all, I've had a good day. I hope this letter finds you well and that you are pleased with my report.

Sincerely, your affectionate "friend,"
Jezebel

I hate the devil, don't you? Jezebel could have written this account of her woman on one of my good days and described me well. Isn't it time for us to wise up? Aren't you ready to put Jezebel on the run?

I most certainly am.

WHO IS SATAN?

I don't know about you, but I was never taught the "who's its" and "what's its" of Satan. I just knew that he existed, that he was very powerful—not as powerful as God but powerful nonetheless—and that I didn't want to mess with him. For the most part I knew very little. And I think Satan liked it that way. When we don't know our Enemy, we might imagine him to be much worse than he is. On the flip side, when we don't know our Enemy, we might underestimate his power and disregard his evil intent altogether. This is what E. M. Bounds warned us not to do. I quoted him in chapter 4, and since he said that "it cannot be said too often" I will repeat it here. "The life of a Christian is warfare, an intense conflict, a lifelong contest. It is a battle fought against invisible foes who are ever alert and seeking to entrap, deceive, and ruin the souls of men."

I was blindsided by Satan three weeks ago because I erred on this side of ignorance. I underestimated Satan's power and disregarded his evil intent. But my husband told me the other day that there is a difference between ignorance and stupidity. When one is ignorant, he simply *doesn't* know. But when he's stupid he *can't* know. I was ignorant, but I'm not stupid. You might be ignorant too, but if you read on you will not be ignorant anymore. In this chapter I am going to tell you who Satan is.

- Satan is a "fallen star."
- Satan is a liar.
- Satan is crafty.
- Satan's bait of choice is offense.

SATAN IS A "FALLEN STAR"

Satan made his first appearance in the Bible in the garden of Eden. I did a bit of research on the origin of Satan and discovered that the Bible has little to say regarding Satan's beginning. We know that he and about a third of heaven's angels were cast out of heaven when Satan led a rebellion against God. (See Revelation 12:3–4; the dragon represents Satan and a third of the stars represents a third of the angels.) And we know that Satan's rebellion was motivated by pride:

> Shining morning star, how you have fallen from the heavens! You destroyer of nations, you have been cut down to the ground. You said to yourself: "I will ascend to the heavens; I will set up my throne above the stars of God. I will sit on the mount of the [gods'] assembly, in the remotest parts of the North. I will ascend above the highest clouds; I will make myself like the Most High." But you will be brought down to Sheol into the deepest regions of the Pit.
>
> ISAIAH 14:12–15 HCSB

John described the battle in more detail in Revelation 12:7–9:

> And there was war in heaven, Michael and his angels waging war with the dragon. The dragon and his angels waged war, and they were not strong enough, and there was no longer a place found for them in heaven. And the great dragon was thrown down, the serpent of old who is called the devil and Satan, who deceives the whole world; he was thrown down to the earth, and his angels were thrown down with him.
>
> REVELATION 12:7–9 NASB

The fact that Satan and his demons rebelled against God tells us that angels have free will. Here are some quick facts about angels:

Angels were created by God—most likely before "in the beginning."

> For by Him all things were created, both in the heavens and on earth, visible and invisible, whether thrones or dominions or rulers or authorities—all things have been created through Him and for Him.
>
> COLOSSIANS 1:16 NASB

Scripture tells us that angels are stronger and wiser than people. Jesus implied they had supernatural knowledge but not unlimited knowledge in Matthew 24:36. Their supernatural power is referenced in 2 Peter 2:11.

> But the exact day and hour? No one knows that, not even heaven's angels, not even the Son. Only the Father knows.
>
> Matthew 24:36 The Message

> However, angels, who are greater in might and power, do not bring a slanderous charge against them before the Lord.
>
> 2 Peter 2:11 HCSB

There are thousands of angels. Many times in Scripture this is mentioned: Deuteronomy 33:2; Psalm 68:17; Matthew 26:53; Hebrews 12:22; Revelation 5:11 to name a few.

> God's chariots are tens of thousands, thousands and thousands; the Lord is among them in the sanctuary as He was at Sinai.
>
> Psalm 68:17 HCSB

> Or do you think that I cannot appeal to My Father, and He will at once put at My disposal more than twelve legions of angels?
>
> Matthew 26:53 NASB

Angels have spiritual bodies and they inhabit spiritual realms—as opposed to the earthly realm created for us. But they do take on the form of physical bodies when sent on human errands (Gabriel visiting Zechariah and Mary, the angel at the tomb, etc.).

The purposes of angels include

- Praising and glorifying God continually before His throne (Revelation 5:11–12; 7:11; 8:1–4).
- Revealing and communicating God's message to people (Luke 1:13–20, 26–38; Acts 8:26; 10:3–7; 12:7–11; 27:23–24).

- Ministering to believers. This includes physical protection but mostly ministering to our spiritual needs. "Angels take great interest in the spiritual welfare of believers, rejoicing at their conversion (Luke 15:10) and serving them in their needs (Hebrews 1:14). Angels are spectators of our lives (1 Corinthians 4:9; 1 Timothy 5:21) and are present within the church (1 Corinthians 11:10). At the death of believers, they convey them to the place of blessedness (Luke 16:22)."[1]
- Executing judgment on the enemies of God.[2]
- Being involved in the second coming of Christ.[3]

Now, keep in mind that Satan was an angel before he was the devil. On Sunday morning one of our pastors gave me this note to encourage me. It was written on a torn piece of notebook paper (I love notes written on torn pieces of paper!). This is what he wrote: "There is no opposite to God. The devil is an opposite only to the archangel Michael. He is a created being. Remember two-thirds of the angels are on our side!" What a great reminder!

But this also means that Satan and all his demons (a third of the original heavenly host) are . . .

- Created by God.
- Stronger and wiser than people.
- Numerous.
- Spiritual in being (but perhaps able to take on some kind of bodily form).
- Exist in direct opposition to their original purposes.

Satan and all his demons . . .

- Profane the name of the Lord.
- Create confusion in communication between God and people.

- Discourage believers—rejoicing in their mess-ups, creating "felt" needs, occupying a presence in the church when welcomed, but certainly banned at the death of believers.
- Persecute the followers of God.
- Will be destroyed at the second coming of Christ.

Millard Erickson suggests that Satan's rebellion most likely took place somewhere between the time God looked at all He created and declared it "very good" (Genesis 1:21) and when Satan appeared to Eve in the form of a serpent (Genesis 3:1).[4]

SATAN IS A LIAR

I mentioned in chapter 1 that Jesus called Satan the Father of Lies (John 8:44). The first step toward being duped by Satan's lies is to yield to his deception. Satan is a deceiver. Neil Anderson writes,

> If I tempted you, you would know it. If I accused you, you would know it. But if I deceived you, you wouldn't know it. If you knew you were being deceived, then you would no longer be deceived. Eve was deceived and she believed a lie. Deception has been the primary strategy of Satan from the beginning.[5]

Let's go back to Eve in the garden. The following is a fictional visit you and I will have with Eve. We're pretending that we've found her just after she's eaten the fruit and stitched her fig leaves together. She and Adam just had a fight, so they're feeling the full impact of their broken relationship for the very first time. Eve's by herself in the corner of the garden.

A visit with Eve

"Eve! We've been looking for you!" we shout.

"Who are you? Where did you come from? Why are you here?" Eve is startled.

"Never mind all that. You look like you've been crying. What's wrong?" we ask.

"Everything! I've messed up royally. I *knew* not to eat that fruit. Adam told me the very first day that it was off limits. And to tell you the truth, I didn't really mind! I mean, we had all this other delicious food in the garden. . . ." Eve pointed to a fig bush nearby, most likely the same one that she'd taken leaves from to stitch her fancy little cover-up.

"So what happened?" We're still a bit mad at her ourselves considering how she's to blame for PMS and labor pains.

"I don't know . . . the Serpent came, asked me what was wrong with our garden," Eve blubbered, her eyes spilling over with tears.

"He said that?" We're beginning to wonder if our translation of the Bible is the best one.

"Well, not exactly. He just asked me a silly question: 'Did God really say, "You must not eat from any tree in the garden?" ' " Eve admitted.

"Go on." We breathe a sigh of relief, grateful that our Bible got that part right.

"Then . . . oh, I don't know what happened then." Eve wiped at the tears and left another smudge of dirt on her otherwise perfect complexion. "I told him that God certainly didn't say that. God gave us lots of trees from which we could eat! Oh, I just wish I'd left it at that!" Eve starts sobbing.

We sit down beside her and gently offer our shoulders to cry on. She chooses yours. You whisper as you stroke her amazing hair, "But you didn't leave it at that, did you, Eve?"

Eve sits up, looks us both in our faces, and states, "No. No, I didn't. He told me we wouldn't die. I knew it was a lie. Deep inside I knew I could trust God. But he told me that God just wanted to keep us ignorant, that He wanted to keep us 'under control.' He told me that as long as we chose to trust God we would miss out on everything else that life has to offer."

We'd be mad at Eve for being so easily deceived if it weren't for the feeling in the pit of our stomachs that we knew exactly where she'd been with that wicked serpent, for we had been there too.

In Nancy Leigh DeMoss's book *Lies Women Believe*, she outlines forty lies that Satan finds women especially prone to believe. Let me list some of them here:

- God is not really good.
- God doesn't love me.
- I'm not worth anything.
- I can't help the way I am.
- I should not have to live with unfulfilled longings.
- I can sin and get away with it.
- God can't forgive what I've done.
- I have to have a husband to be happy.
- I know my child is a Christian because he prayed to receive Christ at an early age.
- If my circumstances were different, *I* would be different.
- I shouldn't have to suffer.
- I just can't take it anymore.[6]

Has Satan ever tried any of these lies on you? Do I have a witness?! Satan is a liar. When he opens his mouth to speak, he speaks lies.

SATAN IS CRAFTY

One reason Satan's lies are so easy to believe is that they are cloaked in remnants of truth. He crafts tricky lies. Consider Satan's lie in Genesis 3:4–5 from *The Message*:

God knows . . .

That's true, He does. God knows everything.

> God knows that the moment you eat from that tree, you'll see what's really going on.

Was that true? Did Eve lack knowledge before she ate the fruit from that tree? I guess that might be so. After all, the fruit did grow on the "Tree of Knowledge of Good and Evil." But what part of good did Eve not understand? While Eve might have lacked the knowledge of evil, she certainly knew good.

If Eve lacked anything, she lacked the wisdom to keep her distance from the devil. She underestimated his power and overestimated his words.

> God knows that the moment you eat from that tree you'll see what's really going on. You'll be just like God, knowing everything, ranging all the way from good to evil.

Are you beginning to figure this out? Certainly God knows everything; that part was true. God knew that the moment Eve ate from that tree she would see things differently, but she certainly wouldn't see "what was really going on." In fact, her vision was about to be so blurred she wouldn't know whether she was coming or going. Once God confronted Eve about her sin, He began to explain to her how life as she'd known it would never be the same again. He explained briefly how sin would continue to rock her world. She would never be "just like God." In fact, Eve was as much like God before she ate the forbidden fruit as she would ever be. And before Eve ate the fruit she was a whole lot like God. Don't forget that in Genesis 1:26–27 God said,

> "Let us make man *in our image, in our likeness*, and let them rule over the fish of the sea and the birds of the air, over the livestock, over all the earth, and over all the creatures that move along the ground." So God created man *in his own image, in the image of God he created him*; male and female he created them.

But after Eve ate the forbidden fruit she was no longer "like" God. She was a terrible misrepresentation of all that God was and of all that God intended for her to be.

Satan is crafty. I've watched him destroy marriages by creating "innocent" friendships between children's Sunday school teachers. What started out as a God-honoring Christian partnership subtly tiptoed closer and closer toward forbidden fruit until all kinds of irreparable damage ripped two families apart.

Satan is crafty.

SATAN'S BAIT OF CHOICE IS OFFENSE

Following a spiritual battle in my life, a dear friend and prayer partner gave me John Bevere's book *The Bait of Satan*. I recommend that you read this book. In his introduction Bevere writes,

> Anyone who has trapped animals knows a trap needs one of two things to be successful. It must be hidden, in the hope that an animal will stumble upon it, and it must be baited to lure the animal into the trap's deadly jaws.
>
> Satan, the Enemy of our souls, incorporates both of these strategies as he lays out his most deceptive and deadly traps. They are both hidden and baited. . . .
>
> One of his most deceptive and insidious kinds of bait is something every Christian has encountered—offense. Actually, offense itself is not deadly—if it stays in the trap. But if we pick it up and consume it and feed on it in our hearts, then we have become offended. Offended people produce much fruit, such as hurt, anger, outrage, jealousy, resentment, strife, bitterness, hatred, and envy. Some of the consequences of picking up an offense are insults, attacks, wounding, division, separation, broken relationships, betrayal, and backsliding.
>
> Often those who are offended do not even realize they are trapped.[7]

My first real battle with spiritual warfare began with an offense against me. This is the bait Satan used to lure me in. As I tell my story, realize that to be offended is not wrong. There are times when people do you wrong, and to be offended is a natural emotional response to their behavior. However, if you don't deal with the offense you might harbor it, and offense that is harbored develops roots of bitterness. Those roots of bitterness then grow weeds of resentment and weeds of resentment stifle the fruit of the Spirit. See if you can determine where I went wrong in the following battle I'm sharing with you.

We had been at our church for seven years and had enjoyed great success. Our congregation was growing, we enjoyed a sweet spirit of fellowship with one another, and we were big enough to offer my preschool children great programs to feed their growing faith.

I'm not sure how it all started, but one Sunday afternoon one of my best friends pointed her finger in my face and said, "Leighann, your husband is a liar. I can hardly sit still when I see him stand in the pulpit every Sunday and claim to preach God's Word."

Wow! Tom had never lied to me! I was baffled. I didn't have a clue that people felt that way about him. What did he do? When did this start? Where did we go wrong? That was the beginning of my offense but certainly not the end. I could still list the names of the women (and men) who said cruel things to me during the next two years. Though I am tempted, I won't list those names here, of course, but suffice it to say I was hurt.

Several months later, after more than sixty people had left our congregation (our worship pastor called this a "back door revival"), I was still nursing my wounds. I'd carefully harbored my offense, and while I wasn't looking, that offense developed those roots of bitterness. (Just like the potatoes develop roots in my pantry when I hide them under TJ's protein powder and forget they are there.) I'll never forget my friend who shook her finger in my face that

Sunday afternoon. But I'll also never forget the next friend who spoke gently to me one night in the driveway outside my home. We had just started a women's Bible study in my recently converted garage/den, and all the women had gone home except for her. With great sincerity Tracy measured her words carefully and said, "Leighann, how long are you going to cry over the people who left us rather than love on the ones that have remained?" It was a good word. For weeks I had played my offense over and over in my head. I'd wallowed in self-pity and listed all my long hours of service and devotion to the people who left us. I couldn't be genuinely happy about the start of our women's study, the new leaders in our Sunday school, or the future God had for our church because I was too busy looking back and playing the game of "poor pitiful me."

During that season of my life, I gradually worked through my offense and asked God to give me the ability to forgive those who'd offended me. This was not an easy process. I had to force my thoughts away from the wrong that was done to me and crucify any right I had to be angry.

Phillip Fulmer, former coach of the University of Tennessee football team, illustrated this valuable lesson to me in an emotional sideline interview I saw at the end of his final UT football game. When asked if he was angry or resentful toward those who cut his career short, Coach Fulmer told the reporter this about harboring offense: "For me to be bitter would be like drinking poison and expecting my enemies to die." I'm sure that statement did not originate with him, but Coach Fulmer made an impression on me when he said it.

WISER AND STRONGER

In this chapter I've given you a quick lesson on the "who's its" and "what's its" of your Enemy. By now you might be exhausted, but take courage, my friend. Now that you have read this chapter, you are wiser than you were before. Yesterday you might have been like I was last month. You might have been ignorant; perhaps there were some things about the Enemy you did not know. But you are not stupid. Today you know a bit more. Now you know that Satan is a "fallen star." You know that he is a liar (the Father of Lies). You know that he is crafty, and you are fully aware of the fact that Satan's most deceptive bait is offense. We've exposed the Enemy. We've made him stand for just a moment in the light of God's Word, and we now have a better idea of what we're battling against.

Who My Enemy Is

Satan is a formidable foe; that is certain. But he's defeated as well. And you and I have power and authority to whip him every time. Be reminded of this truth:

He said to them, "I watched Satan fall from heaven like a lightning flash. Look, I have given you the authority to trample on snakes and scorpions and over all the power of the enemy; nothing will ever harm you. However, don't rejoice that the spirits submit to you, but rejoice that your names are written in heaven."

Luke 10:18–20 HCSB

You are from God, little children, and have overcome them; because greater is He who is in you than he who is in the world.

1 John 4:4 NASB

Underline these verses in your copy of God's Word.

Pray this prayer:

Lord, I understand that you are sovereign, and I know there is none like you. I know that you are almighty, and I trust you. Thank you for revealing these truths to me. Let them soak into my spirit so that I will have wisdom in dealing with the Enemy. Keep me ever mindful that I have authority and power over him—and that he can never harm me. I rejoice that my name is written in heaven and that I am your child. I am an overcomer because you are greater than my Enemy.

SHARPEN YOUR SWORD

God has given you power to overcome. 1 John 4:4
You have authority over the Enemy. Luke 10:19
No weapon formed against you will ever prosper. Isaiah 54:17

Commit the Word to memory: Create a Scripture memory booklet. You can either use index cards and put them together with rings or use a small memo pad–size booklet. While exercising, doing laundry, or waiting for your children's practices to end, read the verses aloud and practice saying them without looking at the words.

Chapter Six

What My Enemy Does

> The thief comes only to steal and kill and destroy; I have come that they may have life, and have it to the full.
>
> John 10:10

When TJ was young I loved to read to him. His favorite book was the one that told the story of David and Goliath. He loved the pictures, and since he was the baby in our family he felt like he could identify with David. I love this story too. In fact, I've written an entire book based on the story of David and Goliath found in 1 Samuel 17 (*Women Overcoming Fear*). In the story of David and Goliath, I have discovered five truths about our Enemy. In the next part of this book I'm going to show you how the Enemy targets the various areas of your life for attack, but first I want you to understand these five truths related to his character. Grab your Bible, open it to 1 Samuel 17, and follow along with me.

TRUTH NUMBER ONE: OUR ENEMY IS AGGRESSIVE

Read 1 Samuel 17:1–3. Note that the Philistines were the aggressors. The Israelites and the Philistines were NOT friendly neighbors.

They had a long history of conflict. But at this particular time, the Israelites were not aggravating the Philistines. The Philistines invaded Israel. "Now the Philistines gathered their forces for war and assembled at Socoh *in* Judah" (verse 1).

In the United States, we are pretty much protected from the invasion of close neighbors. The oceans surrounding us defend us from enemy attack and serve as a buffer from the rest of the world. Unlike us, the countries over the "pond" are separated only by imaginary lines drawn on a map. When I visited Europe a couple years ago, I drove freely across the borders of various countries. But at each border there was a gateway that could be heavily armed and easily transformed from a friendly drive-through welcome center to a bulwark of protection. Europeans have a long history of being invaded and attacked by close neighbors. Just like the Israelites, they have experienced the aggression of their neighbors.

However, the United Sates has not been completely immune to enemy attacks. Even with the oceans protecting us, our enemies have found ways to penetrate our defenses. There are some who still remember the fateful December morning when the Japanese attacked Pearl Harbor. And you can probably still remember exactly where you were and what you were doing when the planes crashed into the World Trade Center in New York City on 9/11.

In the same way that Israel was attacked and our country has been attacked by her enemies, so we—and our churches—are attacked by our spiritual Enemy. Truth number one is this: Our Enemy is aggressive!

Most of the spiritual warfare teaching I've been exposed to focuses on how I can keep myself protected from the attack of this aggressive Enemy. Most often we approach this subject of warfare from the standpoint of "Tell me how I can protect myself!" This need for protection springs out of the experience we've had with an aggressive Enemy. Protection is good. In fact, Paul taught us to clothe ourselves in full battle gear before we even begin to consider going to battle. We would be foolish not to.

In Ephesians 6:13–18 our warfare garb and weapons are listed. They include

- belt of truth
- breastplate of righteousness
- gospel of peace for shoes
- shield of faith
- helmet of salvation
- sword of the Spirit

Great books have been written on the subject of our spiritual armor. One of them is Chip Ingram's *The Invisible War*. Several times in Ephesians 6 Paul wrote that we often win when we "stand firm." Don't forget that victory is sometimes simply not losing ground. There will be times when the Enemy is on the offensive. He will barge into your territory and shake you so firmly that you will do well to refuse to back up. You will defeat him by "standing firm."

But if I only shared with you how to defend yourself against the schemes of the devil, then I would be doing you a disservice. For you were not saved to live a defensive faith. Jesus did not say, "Build a great wall and keep it heavily fortified. Hide behind that wall and huddle together. Be careful to tread softly and stay away from danger, for I am leaving you powerless at the mercy of a formidable foe."

No! Of course he didn't say that! The power that resurrected Jesus from the grave is the power that lives in us today. And that power appropriated through you will send Satan and all his evil companions on the run. Jesus said, "Go and make disciples of all nations. . . . And surely I am with you always, to the very end of the age" (Matthew 28:19–20).

Your Enemy is aggressive. He will find you. But don't think for one minute that simply because he showed up in your life you have to be afraid.

TRUTH NUMBER TWO: OUR ENEMY LOVES TO INTIMIDATE

Read 1 Samuel 17:4–11. Not only did Goliath intimidate the Israelites with his appearance, but he also scared them senseless with his words. Read verses 8–10.

> Goliath stood and shouted to the ranks of Israel, "Why do you come out and line up for battle? Am I not a Philistine, and are you not the servants of Saul? Choose a man and have him come down to me. If he is able to fight and kill me, we will become your subjects; but if I overcome him and kill him, you will become our subjects and serve us." Then the Philistine said, "This day I defy the ranks of Israel! Give me a man and let us fight each other."
>
> 1 Samuel 17:8–10

Goliath had the Israelites so worked into a frenzy that day after day they assembled their troops in the valley—only to run like cowards into their tents. Day after day Goliath shouted. He didn't hit anybody, he didn't poke anyone, and he didn't throw spit wads or even slap anyone! The mere thought of what he might be capable of doing was enough to send the Israelite army packing.

I've heard some people say that the devil loves to intimidate us with words (and thoughts). He's just a big mouth. Beth Moore said that he loves to play make-believe. "Satan plays make-believe. He can only pretend because he lost all rights to presume authority over the believer's life when Christ, 'having disarmed the powers and authorities, . . . made a public spectacle of them, triumphing over them by the cross' (Col. 2:15)."[1]

Unfortunately, Satan plays his game well, and intimidation works. Turn the page in your Bible and read 1 Samuel 17:33: "Saul replied, 'You are not able to go out against this Philistine and fight him; you are only a boy, and he has been a fighting man from his youth.' " After hearing Goliath heckle his troops relentlessly for forty long days, even King Saul was convinced Goliath couldn't be defeated.

Keep in mind that Satan has an agenda. His chief aim is to profane the name of the Lord. He does this by targeting God's children for attack. He wants to steal our joy and kill our testimonies. He wants to make a mockery of God, and in his perilous pursuit, he has no regard for the wasted lives he leaves in his wake.

As members of God's church, our chief aim is to proclaim the name of the Lord. We exist to make His name known among the nations—to demonstrate His glory and to share His love with others. We do this by overcoming the giants the Enemy sets in our paths. Today we rarely ever gird ourselves with armor and march to battlefields to be heckled by Philistine warriors. But we do, nevertheless, face similar foes.

Our giants come in the form of marital strife, struggling relationships, adultery, addictions, and divorce. We face bronze-clad warriors called cancer, financial stress, wayward children, and anger in our homes. The shield bearers for these giants march ahead of them delivering depression, panic attacks, unresolved conflicts from our past, and hopelessness in regard to our future. We face Goliaths in the form of parents with Alzheimer's, our own health issues, broken dreams, friends who disappoint, those who gossip, and even our own insatiable desire for material possessions. The list could go on and on. While many of the things I've mentioned are simply the result of sin-stained life, Satan uses them to intimidate us, to distract us, and to cause us to forget who we are in Christ. Therefore, these (and many other difficult situations) fuel the battle.

How is the Enemy heckling you? In chapters 13 and 14 I'm going to discuss practical ways you can defeat the Enemy, but before I leave this subject let me share with you the best way to overcome the Enemy's use of intimidation: God's Word. God has given you His WORD. He is faithful to it. When you are under attack and the size of your giant, his bronze armor, javelin, and spear shaft frighten you, ask God to give you a *word.* When your giant jeers at you with all kinds of false statements and you start believing what he says—when you find yourself running away and trembling in your tent—open your Bible and ask God to give you His *Word.*

Ask Him for a specific *word*, a *word* that speaks *His* truth into your confusion and chaos. God will give you His word. Then He

The Word of God

Some people use the fact that we can take God at His Word to fuel a "name it and claim it" kind of faith. They take verses out of the context of Scripture and wave them around like magic wands with a "hocus pocus," as if God were just waiting for them to tell Him what to do next. When I encourage you to stand firm on the Word of God, I am not endorsing this ridiculous practice.

Become a student of the Bible. Read it with both discipline and delight. As you grow in your love for God, His Word will become more and more personal to you. During your daily Bible reading you will often feel like He fed you personally with His words. Be careful as you lay claim to God's specific promise that you understand the context in which it was first written, and that you submit to the lordship of Christ in your life. When you do this, God will fulfill His Word in you and proclaim His name through your life just as He did in the lives of those we read about in the Bible.

will accomplish His Word in your life. When you trust God to do what only He can do—and stand boldly face-to-face with your giant—His power will silence your Enemy.

INTIMIDATION AND MONSTER CATFISH

There is a place on Normandy Lake that we fondly call Catfish Point. A few years ago my family was water-skiing near this place when we saw fishermen pull in catfish that looked like small sharks and stretched from a man's thigh to the ground when their captors held them up for us to see. Thus the name Catfish Point.

After oohing and ahhing over the monster catfish, our family went right back to skiing. However, we were so preoccupied with teaching one another new tricks that we never noticed that TJ, who was then age six, didn't get back into the water.

A few weeks later we were on our way to the lake when TJ nonchalantly said, "I'm not skiing today."

"Why not?" I asked.

"I just don't want to," he replied. I thought that perhaps he'd taken a big fall the last time he'd skied and just didn't like drinking lake water. So I made sure he didn't feel any pressure from us. "That's okay, TJ. You can just tube today if that's what you want to do."

"No, I don't think I'm going to tube either," he responded.

That was unusual. For some reason adults can't begin to understand, children find great joy in being tossed from side to side and having their skin rubbed raw against the rubber on those gigantic tubes that take up so much room in the boat.

"Why not?" I asked him.

"I just don't want to get in the water today."

"Suit yourself—that just means more time for the rest of us!"

I assumed that after TJ saw what a great time everyone else was having, he'd jump right in and join us. But we all had our turn in the water and TJ sat quietly on the boat. I wondered what changed my little water bug into a landlubber, when suddenly the memory of those huge catfish filled my mind. It dawned on me that TJ must have been frightened by the size of those fish. How was he to know that catfish didn't pose a threat to people?

"TJ, are you scared of the catfish?" I asked. Fear and relief flooded his eyes as he solemnly looked at me and slightly nodded his head.

"You don't have to be afraid of those fish! TJ, catfish are bottom dwellers! They live way down on the bottom of the lake and don't come up to the top! They never attack people. They won't hurt you!" I reassured him.

After a little more coaxing and some less-than-merciful teasing by his sisters, TJ finally mustered up his courage and jumped back into the lake. Today he loves water-skiing more than any other sport. He slaloms, skis barefoot, and enjoys wakeboarding. When I see him out there on the water, I can't help but wonder what fun he might have missed had he given in to his fear of the monster catfish.

Aren't we like that? Don't we spiritually come face-to-face with some monster catfish and decide to stay out of the water? Satan uses intimidation as his advance guard. If Satan can keep us out of his business of wrecking God's business, he never even has to worry about being obviously evil. God created you for *good works*. God custom-made those plans with you in mind. The giants you face are strategically placed in your path to distract you from fulfilling the *good work* God prepared beforehand for you to do.

You are full of WONDER! You have love to share that will heal broken hearts. You have gifts to give that will lead others to Jesus. You have experiences and talents, passions and drive to literally change the world for the glory of God. Don't be intimidated by bottom dwellers—or as Tom likes to call them, mud-suckers. The giants your Enemy brings against you are no more a threat to your well-being than the catfish that intimidated TJ at Normandy Lake.

Since that time we've skied successfully for years and have yet to treat even one catfish bite!

When Satan heckles you with a bronze-clad blubbering bag of bluff, respond boldly with the powerful promises of God.

TRUTH NUMBER THREE: OUR ENEMY PLAYS DIRTY

Once David arrived on the battlefield, he immediately called the enemy's bluff. David saw Goliath differently than the soldiers saw him, mostly because David saw himself differently than the Israelite soldiers saw themselves. I'll explain this truth completely in chapter 11. But for now I want you to see how the Enemy plays dirty.

Read 1 Samuel 17:26–29. David asked the men standing near him what would be done for the soldier brave enough to take Goliath down. The soldiers told him all about the incentives Saul had offered to that man. But in verse 28, when Eliab, David's eldest brother, heard David's conversation with the other soldiers, he "burned with anger" and asked,

> Why have you come down here? And with whom did you leave those few sheep in the desert? I know how conceited you are and how wicked your heart is; you came down only to watch the battle.

Wouldn't you like to have a big brother like that? (You might have a big brother or sister like that!) Don't forget that when the prophet Samuel came to take a look at Jesse's sons, even Samuel thought surely Eliab would be God's chosen king. To human eyes Eliab looked like a king. But God told Samuel,

> Don't judge by his appearance or height, for I have rejected him. The Lord doesn't see things the way you see them. People judge by outward appearance, but the Lord looks at the heart.
>
> 1 Samuel 16:7 NLT

Can you imagine what kind of jealousy must have fed Eliab's heart when his baby brother was chosen over him to be king?! Can you imagine the snide remarks Eliab might have made toward David that very day? Can you imagine how many times Eliab might have taken the opportunity to put David down, criticize him, and try to embarrass him in front of others ever since that day? This wasn't the first time Eliab had spoken down to David.

Note David's response: "Now what have I done?" (1 Samuel 17:29). Sounds to me like a response from someone who's been rebuked and ridiculed before.

Our Enemy plays dirty. If he can't get us distracted by intimidation, then he'll look for the weak chink in our armor and try to penetrate us where it hurts. He'll find our greatest insecurity and try to expose it.

David was a warrior—not a shepherd boy. He had warrior in his blood. David was destined for greatness. I've no doubt that deep in the secret places of David's heart, he knew this was true. And what David had known in his heart was confirmed by Samuel the prophet, the same man who anointed King Saul. David was a *king* in a shepherd boy's costume! But only David and apparently Samuel knew it. That must have been difficult for David. It must have been difficult to be faithful in the small things (protecting his father's sheep) while he waited for the BIG things he was destined to do. I would imagine this was David's sore spot. It was the stuff that he wrestled with in his prayer time. It was the kind of thing that kept him awake at night.

The very thing that bothered David most was the secret the enemy chose to expose. Satan will always target your sore spot. If your knee is hurt, he'll kick you in your knee. If you are especially sensitive about your appearance, the well-being of your children, your husband's success, your work, or a distant dream—then you can be sure that is where he will target you for attack.

What are you to do about that? Read David's response to Eliab in 1 Samuel 17:30: "He then turned away to someone else and brought up the same matter, and the men answered him as before."

When the Enemy plays dirty and even uses a close friend or family member to rub you where you hurt, do what David did and "turn away to someone else." Stay focused on what God has told you to do. Sometimes you win your greatest battles by turning away from the Enemy's distraction and staying focused on what God has called you to do.

TRUTH NUMBER FOUR: OUR ENEMY TEMPTS US TO PUT OUR CONFIDENCE IN OUR FLESH

Read 1 Samuel 17:38–39. When David finally pressed through the ranks of the army and gained an audience with Saul, Satan's last attempt to defeat David was to convince him that he needed help from something other than God.

Saul might have said, "Okay—you can trust God to protect you. And although none of us think you can do it, we'll let you give it a try. But, please, just for your own sake (and to trick the troops into believing it's me and not you who has collected the courage to take Goliath on), put on my armor!"

Out of respect for his king, David put Saul's armor on. Only, King Saul's armor didn't fit David. Listen, my friend: The world's answer will never fit God's children. When you want to take your giant down, you best not depend on manmade armor.

David responded to Saul, "I cannot go in these. . . . I am not used to them." David could not face Goliath wearing another man's armor. He had to fight his giant with the weapons he'd developed the skill to use, regardless of how inadequate they may have seemed to the professional soldiers or the king in this case.

I have taken some giants down—only to be defeated by others. Why? Because somewhere along the way I started believing what others said about me. I started thinking that my own experience and expertise were somehow responsible for what only God can do.

The minute you forget where your power originates is the minute you profane (rather than proclaim) the name of the Lord. Don't fall for the temptation to put your confidence in anything other than the power of God. A great passage to commit to memory is this:

> His pleasure is not in the strength of the horse, nor his delight in the legs of a man; the Lord delights in those who fear him, who put their hope in his unfailing love.
>
> Psalm 147:10–11

TRUTH NUMBER FIVE: OUR ENEMY IS ALREADY DEFEATED

Goliath was defeated already. First Samuel 17:26 states this truth. I will go into more detail about this in chapter 11. When Jesus died on the cross, Satan's power was stripped away. So why does he remain so active today? Satan knows that once you belong to God he can never take your soul to hell, but he can render you ineffective in snatching other souls from him in his effort to take as many people as he can to hell with him. Basically Satan is a sore loser. You'd better believe the devil is all about stealing your testimony, killing your joy, and destroying your spirit in the process. Jesus warned us about his evil intent in John 10:10. And Peter reminded us that he prowls all over the place seeking to devour us in 1 Peter 5:8.

But remember that these are not two equal but two opposite forces. Satan's power was rendered powerless when Jesus died for you.

What My Enemy Does

Read 1 Samuel 17:45. What three things did Goliath base his confidence in? But WHOM did David place his confidence in? Know *whom* you serve and *what* He promises to do on your behalf.

Pray this prayer:

Father, remind me of my favored position in Christ. Remind me that you have chosen me, and that no matter how often I fail you, you refuse to reject me. Remind me that I have absolutely nothing to fear—for you are with me. I do not need to be dismayed because you are my God. Strengthen me and help me. I know that you uphold me with your righteous right hand. I will not be afraid because your grip never slips. I love you, Lord.

SHARPEN YOUR SWORD

The Lord delights in those who fear Him. Psalm 147:10–11
The Enemy is defeated. Colossians 2:15

Commit the Word to memory: When you choose a verse to memorize, emphasize a different word of that verse each day. When you say the verse aloud, put the emphasis on that word. Do a word study in your quiet time. Do this with each word of the verse until you have the verse committed to memory.

PART THREE

THE TARGETS IN OUR LIVES

The Devil goes out into the wilderness and finds us in a fainting, discouraged condition, with our faith weak, the sky cloudy, and our vision obscured. Then he shows us the world from the loftiest peak of observation, clothed in its most attractive form, and tries to ensnare us with its enchanting wonders. He never gets tired of trying to ruin us.[1]

E. M. Bounds, *Guide to Spiritual Warfare*

Chapter Seven

Satan Targets My Marriage

> "For this reason a man will leave his father and mother and be united to his wife, and the two will become one flesh." This is a profound mystery—but I am talking about Christ and the church.
>
> Ephesians 5:31–32

The Enemy makes his attack gender sensitive. There are five primary targets that attract Satan's aim in women. Four of them have to do with relationships. The devil loves to meddle in our relationships because he knows that God made us relational. We do Bible study together, we eat together, we rear our children together, we pull off our daughters' weddings together, for goodness' sake we even go to the bathroom together! Because we are relational in nature, Satan targets significant relationships for his attack.

The relationship-based targets we will discuss in this book include

- our marriages
- our children

- our friendships
- our churches (The church is always a primary target for Satan because the church poses the biggest threat to his wicked domain.)

I will dedicate a chapter to each of these targets. The other target that we will deal with in this book is our health.

This chapter deals with the first relationship Satan targets for attack, and that is the one you have with your husband. If you are not married, this chapter will address the relationship you have with men in general. For most women this is the most significant relationship in their lives. It is the one that fosters the greatest joy—or the one relationship that fuels the deepest regret.

THE SPIRITUAL SIGNIFICANCE OF MARRIAGE

Why do you suppose the Enemy targets our marriages for attack? In order to understand the spiritual significance of marriage, you need to read Ephesians 5:22–33. Although this is a long passage of Scripture I think that it is worth printing here so that you can see the powerful truth God revealed to us about our marriages:

> Wives, submit to your own husbands as to the Lord, for the husband is head of the wife as also Christ is head of the church. He is the Savior of the body. Now as the church submits to Christ, so wives should [submit] to their husbands in everything. Husbands, love your wives, just as also Christ loved the church and gave Himself for her, to make her holy, cleansing her in the washing of water by the word. He did this to present the church to Himself in splendor, without spot or wrinkle or any such thing, but holy and blameless. In the same way, husbands should love their wives as their own bodies. He who loves his wife loves himself. For no one ever hates his own flesh, but provides and cares for it, just as Christ does for the church, since we are members of His body.

> For this reason a man will leave his father and mother and be joined to his wife, and the two will become one flesh. This mystery is profound, but I am talking about Christ and the church. To sum up, each one of you is to love his wife as himself, and the wife is to respect her husband.
>
> Ephesians 5:22–33 HCSB

Paul wrote some specific instructions to husbands and wives regarding marriage, but then he moved straight from talking directly to husbands and wives to talking about "Christ and the church." Go back through this passage of Scripture and circle every reference Paul made to the church.

In Ephesians 5 God uses a godly marriage to illustrate the love relationship He has with His church. As long as we're living on earth, the best way to see things from God's point of view is to see them with object lessons. When I was a student at Southwestern Seminary, I attended Glenview Baptist Church with my husband. On Sundays, our pastor would deliver a children's sermon. He'd take a seat on the steps that led to the pulpit and invite the children to join him. After the children were assembled around him, he'd often take a brown paper sack and invite the children to guess what he had in his bag. After they'd offered their suggestions, he would pull an object from his bag and then preach a little lesson using the object as his illustration. When Paul spoke of marriage to the church at Ephesus, he was using an object lesson. Think of Ephesians 5 as God's children's sermon for us. God pulls a godly husband and wife from his paper bag. And He says, "See this man, how much he loves his wife? That's how I feel about my church!" Then He points to the wife and says, "See this woman—how she honors her husband and walks hand in hand with him in devotion and service? That's how my church walks with me!"

Can you see why our marriages are critical targets for Satan's attack? If Satan wants to derail God's church, he begins with

A Personal Note to Pastors' Wives

We rose to the top of Satan's list when we married our husbands. Part of our call is to live the message in the spotlight. While all believers are to live their faith, we have a whole lot more eyes watching us. They call it the fishbowl, and I'm not too fond of fish. But nonetheless, when we married ministers we let the Enemy of the cross draw giant X's on our chests. How much greater the damage to God's kingdom when His pastors' marriages fail!

I don't mean for this truth to discourage you, just to sober you. If you are a pastor's wife, realize that one of the greatest ways you can impact God's kingdom work is to love your husband out loud while hundreds of eyes are watching you.

Since the Enemy is determined to wreck your marriage, be wise and embrace the truths in this chapter.

Christian marriages! Satan makes a laughingstock of God's people when he attacks our marriages. When Christian marriages are destroyed Satan says to the world, "See those marriages tearing apart? What God? What church? What does it matter?"

THE ENEMY IS REAL AND THE STRUGGLE IS INEVITABLE

I used to consider myself a failure because I struggled in my marriage. My goal was to live in the "happily ever after" and never, ever even get in a spat. What an unrealistic expectation! It's part of many unrealistic expectations that the Enemy constructs in relationship to marriage.

Satan begins his attack on marriages while we are preschoolers. We nestle closely to someone we love and listen to them read us fairy tales—sweet stories about princesses and princes who live in kingdoms far away and survive great adventures to live . . . "happily ever after." The prince conquers evil foes and the princess has her every wish fulfilled by the handsome, successful prince. The princess is always petite and pretty. When my feet grew to a size 8, I felt an immediate disdain for Cinderella. Why was it that her evil stepsisters had large feet and she had small feet? Why were wicked stepmothers ugly and princesses always pretty? And what was with stepmothers and stepsisters?

I love a story with a happy ending, and I have a solemn vow to only watch movies that end the way I want them to. Life is too full of tragedy for me to be entertained by it! Fairy tales are entertaining, but we need to beware of our "entertainment." Satan uses fairy tales to lay the groundwork for unrealistic expectations in our marriages. This is how he does it: We grow up believing that when we find our charming prince he will satisfy our every need and protect us with diligence until the day we die. What an ingenious way to set women up for failure in marriage! We go into our relationships with boys (who later become men) looking for them to satisfy us in ways they are ill-equipped to do. And our husbands grow up believing they are only as good as the last battle they won. We sit back waiting to be rescued, loved, cherished, and adored, and they have to work and fight and achieve success in order to maintain their "charming" status. Then, of course, there is the whole misconception of "happily" ever after. Who lives that way? It's simply not possible in a sin-stained world!

Satan uses the seemingly innocent fairy tales we learned as children to distort God's plan for marriage. Without thinking twice we whispered "I do" when what we really meant was "He must . . ." Satan attacks our marriages by setting us up to believe that our deepest satisfaction and joy in life can be met by our very own "mister."

The ultimate goal of Christian marriage is much more than personal happiness and bliss. This is the point Paul was making in Ephesians 5. When two Christians marry each other (and Christ followers should marry only Christ followers), God's goal in that marriage is to demonstrate His love relationship with His church. This is not to say that marriage is not satisfying and even a source of deep joy. Satisfaction, joy, and love are gifts God lavishly offers us when we walk in step with Him. These gifts hem us in when we submit ourselves to His purposes and plans. But the primary *purpose* of our marriage is to glorify God.

In learning to battle effectively against the Enemy's attack on your marriage, realize that the Enemy is real and that the struggle is inevitable. Don't set yourself up for failure by embracing the theology of fairy tales. God will gain glory in your marriage as you die to self and look to Him to meet your deepest needs.

WHO YOUR ENEMY IS NOT

Your enemy is not your husband. According to Ephesians 6:12, our struggle is not against flesh and blood. We struggle against the "spiritual forces of evil in the heavenly realms."

Countless people have suffered the heartache of divorce. I've no doubt that many of you reading this book have journeyed down the painful path of divorce. And for those who haven't experienced divorce personally, you have family members or friends whom you've walked beside on that dismal trail. In every divorce there is a period of time that lapses between the day the divorce papers are served and the day the court finalizes the plan. While those papers are waiting in the court system they are titled "Smith vs. Smith" or "Brown vs. Brown" or "Langford vs. Langford" or "he vs. me." Somewhere in the two, or seventeen, or thirty-five years of marriage, the Enemy convinced him and her that their struggle was against flesh and blood.

Oh, how many times have I done the same thing? If we're not careful, we'll lose the battle for our marriages by allowing the devil to suck us into the LIE that our enemy is our husband! Satan will first try to get you to believe the lie that all your discomfort, despair, disappointment, and discouragement are his fault—as if he were ever powerful enough to meet your every need. My friend, your husband is not your enemy!

For those of you who are single: Satan's twist on this lie for you is that a husband would fulfill your heart's desires. With him you would enjoy the fulfillment of most of your longings. He would comfort you, please you, encourage you, and save you from loneliness, despair, and grief. Husbands are good at that some of the time. But at other times they are the ones who cause you despair and grief! Only God can do these things for you.

WHO YOUR ENEMY IS

Your Enemy is a ruler, an authority, a power of this dark world, and a spiritual force of evil who resides in the heavenly realms (see Ephesians 6:12). Go back to chapter 5 and be reminded of who your Enemy is.

Our struggle is real! We have an Enemy who is intent on wrecking our homes. But he is not mortal. He is not made of flesh—he doesn't squeeze the toothpaste meticulously from the bottom of the tube and make mention of the fact that you refuse to do that. My husband could say, "She doesn't leave half-empty coffee cups all over the house."

The Enemy can wound you, but he cannot cripple, disable, or destroy you. The Enemy is strong, but God is stronger. Don't ever forget that the thorns Satan uses to pierce you are the very same ones God can use to increase humility, faith, perseverance, and Christ-like character in you (see 2 Corinthians 12:7–10).

When Satan attacks your marriage, he might wound you, but he can never destroy you. The Enemy is defeated. Don't forget this. Anything God can be glorified in—Satan is against. The marriage relationship is a mirror of Christ's relationship with the church. This relationship, when it is healthy and God-honoring, provides the world with a snapshot—a visual image, a physical illustration—of Christ's love for and relationship with His bride, the church.

THE MOST POWERFUL THING YOU CAN DO

The most powerful thing you can do to win the battle for your marriage is this: *Pray with your husband every single day*.

At our church we host a CPR (Couples Praying Regardless) emphasis every year between Mother's Day and Father's Day. During this time we invite husbands and wives to pray together on a daily basis. We provide tools to help them, and we celebrate their successes by sharing testimonies. We've had more amazing things happen in the marriages in our church through this prayer emphasis than we have had happen through any other marriage enrichment programs that we have offered.

Take a look at some marriage facts and figures Amy Desai compiled for Focus on the Family[1]:

> While the divorce rate in America has leveled off and even decreased slightly in the past few years, the divorce rate is still twice as high as it was in 1960.[2] It's estimated that for couples marrying today, the lifetime probability of divorce or separation remains between 40 and 50 percent before one partner dies, although this percentage is significantly lower for those who marry after age 21, graduate college and are religiously committed.[3] More than one million children a year experience their parents' divorce.[4] And a recent survey reported that the divorce rate among Christians is now the same as or higher than in the broader culture.[5]

Even if only one Christian couple were to experience divorce, that would be too many. Children of the King can win this battle. The following quote shows that even the statistics prove that God equips you to win the battle for your marriage.

> The often-cited statistic that 50 percent of marriages end in divorce—even among churchgoers—can make commitment seem fruitless. But that statistic is misleading. Dozens of studies distinguish between couples who claim a nominal faith and those who prioritize church attendance. *Couples who have a strong commitment to faith and attend church regularly are far more likely to have lifelong relationships*.
>
> *One recent study in particular shows that those who go to church and pray together have a much lower divorce rate*. The University of Virginia's Brad Wilcox found that regular church attendance cuts the likelihood of divorce by 30 percent to 35 percent. . . .
>
> While that rate is still unfortunately high, when you add prayer into the mix, thoughts of divorce plummet. A 1998 survey by the Georgia Family Council found that among couples who prayed together weekly, only 7 percent had seriously considered divorce, compared to 65 percent of those who never prayed together. [6]

The first year I challenged the couples in our congregation to pray together daily, I said,

> Do you remember the phrase the pastor said at your wedding? "What God hath joined together, let no man separate." God knows how to keep His marriages together. Unfortunately, too often we don't let Him have this victory because we don't pray. Second Chronicles 7:14 says, "If my people, who are called by my name, will humble themselves and pray and seek my face and turn from their wicked ways, then will I hear from heaven and will forgive their sin and will heal their land [homes]."

Throughout the years we've adapted and adjusted the way we practice our CPR emphasis each year, but we still practice it and have had incredible success in helping husbands and wives grow closer to God and to one another by learning to pray together. Here is one testimony from this experience:

> Hi, Leighann,
>
> The day you gave the challenge for us to pray together as couples, I thought, *Well, I guess I will be praying with my kids*. Being a spiritually single wife, I just knew that I could not ask my husband to pray with me. He would just think that I was crazy!
>
> So, I committed to pray with my kids.
>
> Then in our Sunday school class some of the women were sharing how they had prayed with their husbands, and I thought, *Wow . . . I didn't even try to pray with mine*. So I decided to ask him to pray with me, and guess what . . . he did! Well, he didn't pray; I did (and cried a lot too). It was such an awesome experience and I know he felt the Holy Spirit move that day. I know that God is working on my husband through our boys and all the wonderful people at our church. I am so thankful for all the prayers for my husband.
>
> In June I felt it was time for me to move to a new Sunday school class. God wants me to be in a class that my husband can attend with me. So I moved. This week my husband committed that he would come to this class with me. God is so good! I would never have dreamed that he would go with me to a class. He has told me that going to church would be okay but that he would not go to a class.
>
> I am writing this letter with tears of joy. Please keep him in your prayers, especially this week, that God will do things in Kendall's heart he has never known before.
>
> Stacey

A few months after that year's CPR emphasis Kendall came to know the Lord and surprised his wife by appearing in the baptistery during a morning worship service. Today Kendall and Stacey serve God faithfully through our church. Their older son is in New Zealand with a team of summer missionaries, and their youngest son just returned home from a mission trip to Mazatlan, Mexico.

This is just one of many testimonies I could share with you of marriages that have been transformed by prayer. If you want to win the battle for your marriage, pray with your husband daily.

HE'S NOT ALL THAT

I hope to write another book on this subject of men and marriage someday. It will be titled *He's Not All That!*

Too many women put too much stock in the ideal of marriage. Don't get me wrong, marriage is wonderful! I'm married to my best friend, my lover, my partner in life. Tom is great! But marriage is also awful. I'm also married to a man who has wounded me deeply, sorely disappointed me, and failed me on many occasions. Tom is terrible!

For those of you who have never married, it's not all you might think it should be. If you are driven by a deep conviction that only a husband will complete and fulfill you, then you are being deceived by the Enemy. If you are looking for a man who is pretty close to perfect, maybe you should submit your "Top Ten List" to God and let Him give you what He knows is best rather than wander for years on a treasure hunt for someone who doesn't even exist. Just be sure that "madly in love with Jesus" stays number one on your list. For without Christ at the center of your relationship, you won't even get close to what God has in mind for you.

For those of you who are sorely disappointed in your man, for those who married before you knew to wait for God's direction, and for those who are married to men who don't love the Lord—be encouraged! God knows where you are, and He is perfectly able to meet your needs—especially the ones your man can't figure out.

For all of you, release those men from having to be what only God can be in your life. The lie that has wrapped itself around the minds of women today is the lie that Prince Charming has to meet needs that only God can meet. Just as the devil told Eve that God was holding out on her—so he tells women today that God is failing to give you something you desperately need in relationship to marriage.

In his book *When the Enemy Strikes*, Charles Stanley lists the needs that people experience. He breaks them up into three categories: physical, emotional, and spiritual. The physical needs include food, water, air, and security. Emotional needs include human love and acceptance; feelings of competency, praise, or recognition that lead to feelings of worthiness; and purpose or usefulness. The spiritual needs include God's unconditional love, God's forgiveness of sins, the assurance of everlasting life, and an awareness of God's abiding presence that gives hope for the future and confidence that God is always in control.[7]

Stanley goes on to explain that God can meet every one of these needs. This is what he says concerning our emotional needs.

> God can meet all of your emotional needs. He does this directly through the abiding presence of the Holy Spirit in your life. He also does this by sending people into your life who can wrap their arms around you and love you, encourage you, build you up, applaud you, and help you discover your unique gifts and ways in which to use them for the greatest good—now and in eternity.[8]

Watch for those people! They are more than one man. Your husband may be one of them, but he is certainly not all of them. Become that person to others. God is capable of meeting all your needs. The devil will use your "neediness" to weaken your defenses and initiate his attack. He accomplishes this often in the lives of women, especially in relationship to the men they love. Satan whispers lies like these:

"You need a man to erase your loneliness."

"A man will complete you."

"If only your husband understood you better, then he would know how to help you."

"Your man isn't right for you. He doesn't even care!"

And the list goes on and on. Be careful to realize that God is willing and able to meet ALL your needs. He will meet them through multiple people and in multiple ways. This promise is solid. God's given you His word. "And my God will supply *all* your needs according to His riches in glory in Christ Jesus" (Philippians 4:19 HCSB).

Satan Targets My Marriage

If you are married, pray with your husband today.

Read Ephesians 5:22–33 again and then pray this prayer if you are married:

Father, forgive me for being so selfish in my marriage. Forgive me for thinking more about what I need and what I expect than I think about how you are glorified in my relationship with my husband. Thank you for being patient with me. Help me to find a way today to encourage my husband. And grow us to be a great picture of your loving relationship with your church.

Pray this prayer if you are not married:

Father, thank you for being a husband to me. Thank you for fulfilling all my needs. Forgive me for looking to others for what only you can give. Help me to be the arms of love and the voice of encouragement in the life of another. Show me someone who is lonely and hurting today and prompt me to love them in the same way that you love your church. I trust you to fulfill my every need according to your glorious riches in Christ Jesus.

SHARPEN YOUR SWORD

God knows how to keep your marriage strong. Ephesians 5:22

God promises to meet your every need. Philippians 4:19

God is able. Ephesians 3:20

Commit the Word to memory: As a way to encourage your prayer time with your husband, start memorizing Scripture together. Choose a verse a week (or a verse a month) and pray your verse. Then practice saying the verse to each other.

CHAPTER EIGHT

Satan Targets My Children

"As for me, this is my covenant with them," says the Lord. "My Spirit, who is on you, and my words that I have put in your mouth will not depart from your mouth, or from the mouths of your children, or from the mouths of their descendants from this time on and forever," says the Lord.

ISAIAH 59:21

MIKEL MADE ME A MOTHER

We watched the monitor. As the next contraction came, Tom and Amy shouted with the gusto of a crowd of college football fans, "PUSH!" Where did all this pushing come from? I thought that since I gave in to the wiser, wimpier choice to have an epidural, Mikel was to arrive with little difficulty and no pain. Since when did babies take so much coaxing to get here?

But here we were, at 11:00 p.m. . . . PUSH!

I'm pushing already. I'm not an out-of-shape person. In fact, just yesterday I swam a mile at the YMCA pool. I think Tom must have been sharing my thoughts because somewhere in between the commands to push I heard him say, "Amy, how high have you ever seen that mark go when a woman pushed?" He was referring to the monitor that draws a picture of your contractions. Mine was looking like a graph presented to the board of directors mapping the sale of corn chips in the southeastern states over the last six months. In the midst of breathing, I halfheartedly listened to this conversation, afraid of where it was headed. Amy replied, "Oh, I don't know, about right here I guess." She pointed to a spot slightly higher than corn chip sales in July.

My husband is a wonderful man. He'd already gained my admiration for hanging with me during some rather uncomfortable infertility procedures. He'd cleaned up grape juice freshly regurgitated on the new carpet in our bedroom during those early days after discovering Mikel would be coming. He'd even stopped mentioning that I only weighed a pound or so less than he did. But even in all these admirable "in sickness and in health" accomplishments, Tom is very competitive. He played college tennis and won many times due to his sheer determination. Everything he did somehow turned into a competition. The question about the highest mark was loaded. And here came the next command: "PUSH, Leighann! You can do it! Go higher! PUSH! Nobody can push like you can! Yeah, you can do it!" Had you been there, you would've thought we were in the birthing babies' event at the Pan American Games! And in obedient, determined response, PUSH I did . . . for another forty-five minutes.

It was now 11:45 p.m. Enter Dr. Growdon. "How are we doing?"

Fine, just fine. I've survived four months of the worst nausea of my life. I faithfully jogged, then walked and swam to keep my body in shape. I attended all those inconvenient childbirth classes (even though I apparently slept through the pushing part), and I stepped on those dreaded scales every time I went to your office. Then I lay still while you poked and prodded, I only winced a little when they blew up my vein while inserting the needle for the IV, and I prayed through the dreaded epidural. Now I've BEEN PUSHING FOR AN HOUR AND A HALF! How am I doing? Fine, of course I'm fine!

Although I'd already more than defeated any other woman in the pushing competition, Mikel didn't seem to get any closer to her goal of entry into this world. By now, even I—the Olympic swimmer—had had enough. The tears started to flow, "Tom, I can't. I can't push anymore. She just won't come."

Dr. Growdon called for the vacuum. Now I could push and he could pull. At least that was the plan, but upon seeing the threatening-looking instrument and feeling some hard-to-ignore contractions, my second wind came strong. The next contraction came and now I had a choir of coaches: Tom, Dr. Growdon, the anesthesiologist, Amy (my nurse), another nurse there to assist who knows who, and—just outside the door—my mother-in-law, father, mother, and sister all in one accord, "PUSH!"

And with a few more great efforts Mikel came. It was 12:08 a.m., March 12, 1992. The Pan American Games were over, and suddenly the stadium grew quiet. Mikel Lorin McCoy was here. They laid her in my arms. As I gingerly took her, my hands shook and my eyes filled with tears. At that moment I didn't even remember pushing. All I knew was that somehow, some way God blessed me beyond measure, and now after years of yearning, hoping, pleading, crying, and growing, Leighann McCoy was a mother.

Never before had seven pounds, eight and three-quarter ounces felt so heavy. As she looked at me I smiled between tears. Though my mouth couldn't make a sound, my heart cried out to God, "How on earth will I ever be able to love her enough? How will I teach her your ways? How will I be her mother? Oh, God, how will I lead her to become all you've already purposed for her to become? How will I endure her pain? How can I guide her to choose you above all else? What responsibility is mine! What an overwhelming burden is mine."

A MOTHER'S HEART

I thought I knew myself well before Mikel was born. I thought I knew what aggravated me, what might make me cry, and what brought me great joy. My heart and I had been gentle companions for twenty-eight years. I knew what kind of marriage I wanted to have with Tom—and what goals I wanted to accomplish. I knew what I liked to do for fun and who I liked to do it with. I even knew how to handle disappointment and where to go for encouragement.

But when the doctor laid my seven-pound-eight-and-three-quarter-ounce answered prayer in my arms, suddenly all that vanished. The heart I was familiar with was immediately replaced by one that seemed foreign to me. This new "mother heart" beat much stronger. It was as if my entire chest shook with each thump. When I looked into her curious eyes, my gigantic heart ached with both indescribable joy and wordless pain.

I was a MOTHER! And with one little bitty bundle of joy I had a whole new heart to deal with. It's a vicious thing, this mother's heart. Only by utter determination has it not taken out a coach or two! Only by the grace of God has it managed to navigate the white water rapids of her tears and resist the temptation to keep those tears from falling at all costs. And oh, how it still thumps today, shaking my entire frame when she has experienced genuine joy.

That mother heart tripled in size with the arrival of Kaleigh and TJ. Over and over my mother heart has swelled with joy and shattered with grief. It is doing both as I write this book. You mothers know what I'm talking about, don't you? Where once you might have been timid, suddenly you have the ability to assert yourself like a mother grizzly bear! There's no limit to what a mother heart might do.

The second relationship the Enemy targets for attack is the one we have with our children. One of Satan's favorite places to pour on the lies is in the world of motherhood. In the conferences I lead I ask for a show of hands. "How many of you would say you are an excellent mother?" Very few women raise their hands. But when I ask, "How many of you have ever had this thought: '*I am a terrible mother*'?" almost everyone in the room raises her hand. This goes to show how powerful Satan's attack is toward us in the relationship we have with our children. Two things could be true: Either you are a terrible mother or you are not.

If you really are a terrible mother, stop it! Confess your sin to God, receive His forgiveness, and get help! Jesus forgives sin. And what is even better, God refuses to hold your sin against you. He promises to never bring it up again—ever.

> Therefore, there is now no condemnation for those who are in Christ Jesus, because through Christ Jesus the law of the Spirit of life set me free from the law of sin and death.
>
> Romans 8:1–2

If you are a mother who has knowingly harmed your child—or children—I want you to pray this prayer aloud right now:

> *Lord, I am sorry for (whatever you have done as a mother to harm your child[ren]). I humbly ask you to forgive me for (whatever you did). I realize that Jesus died for this sin too. I receive your forgiveness. I renounce the thoughts that plague me with shame. I profess that I am a beautiful, clean, and pure daughter of the King of Kings and Lord of Lords. And I am free to be the very best mother you want me to be through the power of your Holy Spirit working in and through me. I am committing right now to seek help so that I can be the very best mother you want me to be. In Jesus' name I pray. Amen.*

If you prayed that prayer, you are forgiven. Celebrate the fact that God knows how to help you change. Seek wise people God might use to help you become the mother your children need.

Most of us are not nearly as terrible as our Enemy accuses us of being. If you really aren't a bad mother, that voice of slimy accusation comes from your Enemy to distract and discourage you. Don't let the devil get away with heckling you in this area of your life. God knows your heart. And He knows your limitations. You will make mistakes, but rarely ever are they mistakes of the heart.

A few weeks ago I was crying over my current child-related crisis, and my mind wandered back to the days when I was infertile. For three years I begged God to give me a baby, and while I was whining and crying I was certain I'd be the best mother ever. Until May 31 of this year, I was fairly satisfied in Tom's and my parenting skills. I always said, "The proof is in the pudding," but I firmly believed that all three of my children were on the right track.

As I cried out to God this summer, my despairing thoughts wondered why He ever let me be a mother at all. I confessed to Him that I messed up royally, and that my mistakes helped pave the way for hers. The Enemy was condemning me. But he didn't condemn for long. For I remembered this truth I've been teaching for years:

I am her mother. Good, bad, or indifferent, I'm the one God chose for her. I may feel inadequate, I will make mistakes, and I may beg for do-overs. But when the dust settles in the aftermath of her growing up—I'll still be God's chosen mother for her. If I do a good job, then "Yay, God!" He blessed her with a good mother. When I do a poor job, then I need to cling to God, being thankful for the reminder that only He can be perfect for me, and for her.

Even when I make mistakes, I'm still God's perfect mother for both my daughters and my son. Today I rest in that truth and encourage you to do the same. Even if you are one of the mothers who prayed and asked God to forgive you for hurting your child (knowingly or unknowingly), realize that you are God's perfect mother for him or for her. God will show you how to depend on Him to move forward from here.

BE SMART!

Here are some practical things you can do to win the battle for your children. Be SMART! Second to wrecking your marriage, there is no greater victory Satan has in a Christian family than to destroy your children. Therefore, recognize that they are at risk and be SMART!

S—SET BOUNDARIES AROUND YOUR KIDS

Set a boundary around what they experience. I used to steer my son away from toys that mimicked monsters and books or movies that dealt with occult subjects. I would say, "You cannot play with that because you are a child of the King!" I tried to explain to him that royal children—heirs to the throne—are not reared like paupers. They are reared differently because there is great responsibility and purpose waiting to unfold in them. TJ still didn't like the fact that he grew up with more restrictions than some of his classmates, but I hope I instilled in him a sense of connection with God's destiny for his life.

Set a boundary against your own expectations and those of others. Our children sense pressure from us when their behavior makes us proud or humiliates us. They sense this detrimental pressure when we fall into the trap of reliving our own childhoods through them. That's a lot of pressure. Realize that your sons and daughters will be who they are. They will make their own choices—some will be good and some will be bad. They will navigate their own paths through life. When they make you proud, humbly smile—and let them own their accomplishment. When they disappoint or embarrass you—remember this life lesson is more about them and their future than it is about you and your past. Pray for them and love them through their mistakes. Don't wrap your own self-image around their choices. And don't let others do that to them.

M—MANAGE YOUR HOUSEHOLD WELL

I've learned that if I can keep some semblance of order in my home, my children are more secure and better equipped to combat the battles they face away from home. For instance, TJ used to go berserk if he didn't have clean socks in his dresser drawer in the morning. I realized that clean socks translated: "I'm taken care of here. While I'm not sure what's going to happen 'out there,' here I know that I am loved and I can anticipate my needs being met."

So I invested in socks for TJ. My traveling means lots of socks. While the rest of the family has ten pairs or so, TJ has maybe forty pairs of socks. Clean socks result in a great day. TJ has grown out of the clean sock phase. Now he's into clean white T-shirts. It's all he ever wears! While the other boys need expensive, name-brand shirts to feel cool, my son sports Fruit of the Loom! He's also grown past the stage of Mom doing his laundry. Now when his T-shirts and socks are dirty, he just puts a load of laundry in to wash before he goes to bed and comes down to transfer it to the dryer when he gets up. Or he talks his sister into a run to the nearest super center and spends his own money on another bag of T-shirts or socks.

Through the years I've learned that Crock-pots, decent washing machines, and toilet paper in abundance can go a long way in resisting the devil. He may be crafty, but we can head him off with common sense. The Proverbs 31 woman is my inspiration:

> She watches over the affairs of her household and does not eat the bread of idleness. Her children arise and call her blessed; her husband also, and he praises her.
>
> Proverbs 31:27–28

A—ALWAYS BE THEIR ADVOCATE

Even when the whole world is against your children, you be in their court! You be for him! You be for her! I have no doubt this is why many men and women succeed. They know their parents are FOR them!

I have lived the bleacher life. I've been watching my kids play ball for over ten years, and I have to confess, I have never cared how many games we won or lost. I've got one purpose for being in those stands and one purpose only—to watch my child play ball. When she's in the game, I'm watching her. When she's riding the bench, I am watching her. I spent an entire basketball season one year watching TJ watch his team play ball. After countless hours of everybody else's son playing ball, I cheered mine on for the two minutes he dribbled and shot in the one game he played. I am for him! I am for her! And don't ask me to give you an objective assessment of their talent. They are the BEST! The absolute best—don't confuse me with your stats.

When Mikel was a toddler, Tom taught her a little cheer. It went like this: "Daddy, Daddy, Daddy, number one!" She would pump her little arms while she shouted "Daddy," then raise her index finger to the sky when she said, "Number one!"

Last week Tom wrote Mikel a note. In it he reminded her of that little cheer. And as tears streamed down his face he wrote, "Mikel, I know I'm not number one in your life today. And I don't know if you still believe in me. But I want you to know that I believe in you. I'm pumping my arms in the air and raising my index finger to the sky, and I'm shouting, 'Mikel, Mikel, Mikel, number one!' " He stamped and mailed that letter and meant every word that he wrote.

No matter where your children take you, always be their advocate. You don't have to condone their behavior or compromise God's standards, but you can be for him. You can be for her. There might be times when you are the only one who believes in them.

R—RETREAT AND RELAX!

Laughter is good medicine. As families, we need to do silly things together—things that don't matter so much. Sometimes our lives are filled with serious situations. There was a season in our ministry when three young adults and two babies died in a matter of months. When the pressure grows intense we look for ways to retreat and relax.

The absolute *best* investment our family ever made was in our ski boat. It holds only five people, so there's just enough room for us. When we get together in that boat and spend a day on the lake, we can simply be ourselves without the pressure of worrying about what someone else might think of us, what illness might strike tomorrow, or what poor choices might derail us the day after that. You might have other toys you enjoy. And even if your finances are limited, you can still find ways to retreat and relax.

Last year during fall break we made our three kids go with us to the mountains. (Notice that we had to "make them." Enjoy the days when they want to be with you, for those days will not last forever!) We had a blast! TJ became a lumberjack when he chopped down his first tree, Mikel learned to build a fire in a buck stove, and Kaleigh heated apple cider. When I was a child our family went camping. It was an inexpensive way to spend quality time together.

Good times together defeat the devil.

T—TAKE IT EASY

One of Satan's favorite strategies against us is fear and intimidation. Realize that although he may win the skirmish, he ain't ever gonna win the war. When I feel like I'm losing the battle for my children, I simply remember the verse God gave me for their future: "Then our sons in their youth will be like well-nurtured plants and our daughters will be like pillars carved to adorn a palace" (Psalm 144:12).

They are HIS KIDS! And He's got it all under control. God's purposes prevail when we take Him at His Word; when we trust Him, obey Him, and cling to Him. God will take care of His kids!

A WORD OF ENCOURAGEMENT FOR THOSE WHOSE CHILDREN ARE FAR FROM GOD

I never wanted to be an authority on this subject. I sympathized with others but secretly enjoyed the fact that my children would *never* do that. And here I am today. I truly hope that by the time this book goes to print I'll have my victory story to share with you—but even if I don't, I know that day will come. As I follow God on this new trail (a rocky path that seems to be not-so-well groomed), I have learned one powerful truth.

The Enemy wants me to doubt God. He keeps heckling me with all God's promises related to my children. Several years ago God gave me Zephaniah 3:17 specifically for Mikel. I knew God gave this verse to me because I am **never** in Zephaniah. It's the verse I printed at the beginning of chapter 1:

> The Lord your God is with you, he is mighty to save. He will take great delight in you, he will quiet you with his love, he will rejoice over you with singing.

This is God's Word concerning Mikel. As I cling to this Word, the Enemy taunts me: "How is God going to do that now?! She's messed it all up! Her free will has interrupted God's plans! Look at what I am stealing from you. Isn't she your child of promise? Didn't you call her your 'flesh-and-blood proof that God answers prayer'? Look at her now! What do you think of this?!"

And if I'm really willing to be honest with you—I am disappointed. I *hate* what the Enemy has stolen (and continues to steal) from her. I do wonder how God is going to bring glory to himself through *this*. But I'm choosing to cling to God's Word on the situation.

Mikel loves to read fiction. But she has a quirky way of doing it. She always reads the last page before she reads the book. I asked her, "Why do you do that? Doesn't it mess up the story for you?" And she answered, "No! I want to know how the story's going to end before I spend all that time reading the book. If I don't like the ending I know I won't like the book."

I had to smile—she had a point. I don't choose to do that when I read fiction, but I understand. However, in this situation the only way I can function today is to read the last page of the book that God is writing with Mikel's life. I helped write the first few chapters, but she's writing it by herself now. However, God has written the end. And Zephaniah 3:17 is His final word. I find great comfort in that truth.

I encourage you, if you find yourself in my shoes today (or someday), to ask God to show you the last page of the book. Read it carefully. Print it on your heart. Carry it in your purse and trust God to get your baby there. He'll do it—He has to! He's never not kept His Word.

> God is not a man, that he should lie, nor a son of man, that he should change his mind. Does he speak and then not act? Does he promise and not fulfill?
>
> NUMBERS 23:19

Satan Targets My Children

If you haven't already found God's promises in relationship to your children, search for them today.

Here are some promises from Isaiah you might consider:

Isaiah 59:21

Isaiah 46:3–4, 8–10

Isaiah 43:1–3, 18–19

Pray this prayer:

Father, thank you for inviting us to call you that. You are the perfect parent, and you know how to perfectly parent the children you've entrusted to me. I realize that they are not really mine. They are yours and you trusted me with them for a season. Help me to trust you with them when my season is done. I realize that my role as their mother is not really ever finished, but that I will parent them best when I can rest in you. Thank you for my children (name them), and for the promise you have given me for their lives. I love you, and am grateful that you are my Father which art in heaven.

SHARPEN YOUR SWORD

There is no condemnation in Christ. Romans 8:1–2

God expects you to take care of your home. Proverbs 31:27–28

God will pass your faith on through your kids. Isaiah 59:21

Commit the Word to memory: Challenge your family to memorize an entire passage of Scripture. Choose a psalm or one of the verses in this book and give each person a verse or a phrase to commit to memory. When you get together to share a meal, practice saying your verses aloud. First go around the table and let each person quote their portion of the Scripture, then say the entire passage together in unison. This might take a month or longer, but the reward will be great.

CHAPTER NINE

Satan Targets My Friendships With Other Women

> No one has ever seen God; but if we love one another, God lives in us and his love is made complete in us.
>
> 1 JOHN 4:12

The third relationship category that Satan targets for attack is our friendships with other women. My greatest hurt in the ministry came at the hands of other women. For many years I kept other women at a safe distance. I built an invisible fence around my heart and dared anyone to cross it. I grew up in a family with three sisters and decided that I didn't necessarily like girls. They were petty, they gossiped, and they seemed to be in a constant state of competition with one another (not just my sisters, but girls in general). Some of my best friends were guys. So when I married I determined to let one and only one person behind my invisible fence, and that was Tom.

But after several years of marriage I realized that Tom didn't make a very good girlfriend. So I ventured out away from my great wall and risked casual friendships with a few women in our church. I felt like I'd really accomplished my goal of developing friendships with other women when I traveled with five of them to Florida for a few days at the beach. I conquered my fears and allowed some of my casual friends to become trusted companions.

But not long after our beach getaway, one of the very few women who'd made it to the perimeter of "trusted companion" confronted me on a Sunday afternoon. She was the one I mentioned before who said to me, "Your husband is a liar! I can't stand to hear him preach." I was shocked. She, along with my other "friends," had somehow gotten sideways with Tom. This particular Enemy attack had more to do with the church than it had to do with my friendships, but I couldn't help but take her accusation personally. I felt as if she'd taken a knife and thrust it into my back. Over the next few years she and my other "beach buddies" kept wounding me with their suspicions and accusations.

My response to this experience was to reconstruct my invisible fence. But the more I read God's Word the more I realized that I couldn't serve the Lord without loving His people. And I couldn't love His people if I insisted on keeping them away from my heart. God longs for us to love one another. When we love one another we express His love to the world. "No one has ever seen God; but if we love one another, God lives in us and his love is made complete in us" (1 John 4:12).

Satan targets your relationships with other women because there is great testimony in our love for one another. We demonstrate the tremendous love of God when we love one another. Remember, Satan's chief aim is to profane the name of the Lord. If he can keep us at odds with one another, if he can destroy our friendships, then he can profane God's name. Take 1 John 4:12 and consider its opposite:

> No one has ever seen God; and if we refuse to love one another, God will be far from us and his love will never be seen through us. Therefore no one will ever see God.

See what is at stake? Satan consistently pounds away at relationships in our lives. He longs to destroy our marriages, our relationships with our children, and our friendships with other women. I'm not going to exhaust this subject, but I am going to remind you that God made us to be interdependent on one another. When the Pharisee asked Jesus which was the greatest commandment (and remember there were hundreds of commandments by the time the Sadducees and Pharisees had interpreted the ones given to Moses by God), Jesus replied:

> "Love the Lord your God with all your heart and with all your soul and with all your mind." This is the first and greatest commandment. And the second is like it: "Love your neighbor as yourself." All the Law and the Prophets land on these two commandments.
>
> MATTHEW 22:37–40

God commands us to love Him and to love one another.

WHY I NEED GIRLFRIENDS

As women we need other women. Even *if* your girlfriends have let you down, you still need them, and they still need you. Here are four reasons I've discovered I need girlfriends:

1. THERE ARE SOME THINGS ONLY WOMEN UNDERSTAND

Those things include the fact that I *need* chocolate, why the perfect color of nail polish can change my mood almost immediately, and how I can simply look at a piece of cake and gain a pound. Girlfriends understand that telling me not to worry is simply wasting words when it's my daughter who's learning to drive! They also know about PMS and menopause.

There are other things women understand as well. When I discovered my daughter was pregnant, I shared my news with the grandmother of one of Kaleigh's friends. Pam knew exactly what I was feeling because she experienced what I am experiencing some seventeen years ago and has been down this cluttered path before me. Her granddaughter (Kaleigh's friend) is the baby my daughter will one day have! God will help me navigate my way (with the help of my girlfriend Pam) through these troubled waters where Satan would love to win a victory.

My friend Terra has a son who is a senior this year. I love Will. He works hard, plays hard, and is growing toward becoming a mighty man of God. Will had a difficult time last year with his basketball coach. At the same time my son TJ was having a difficult time with basketball. Terra and I consoled each other. We reminded each other that we were rearing men of God, not basketball players. God will bring glory to himself as He allows Terra and me to encourage each other as we stand firm against the attacks the Enemy plots against our sons.

Scripture tells me that God put other women in the world for such times as these!

> Praise be to the God and Father of our Lord Jesus Christ, the Father of compassion and the God of all comfort, who comforts us in all our troubles, so that we can comfort those in any trouble with the comfort we ourselves have received from God.
>
> 2 Corinthians 1:3–4

2. HAVING FRIENDSHIPS WITH OTHER WOMEN TAKES THE PRESSURE OFF MY HUSBAND

Now Tom doesn't have to be my girlfriend, my lover, my confidant, my knight in shining armor, my hero, my pal, my fashion consultant, and my Lillie Belle's lunch date too. In fact, Tom McCoy wouldn't be caught dead in Lillie Belle's. Lillie Belle's was a Victorian house turned sandwich shop where my friend Karen and I solved many world problems. You need to be glad that we met there on a regular basis. The earth might have slipped from its axis had we not scheduled lunch and sipped hot tea. Unfortunately Lillie Belle's was sold and is no longer a lunch destination. But, as divine providence would have it, we now have a similar restaurant right across the street from our church. The Homestead Manor serves high tea by reservation every afternoon—and so you can sleep in peace tonight knowing that Karen and I will take care of the world's problems as we sip peach and ginger tea at the Homestead Manor.

Before I understood the truth that girlfriends take the pressure off my husband, I expected far too much from Tom. I wanted him to *want to* listen and to *want to* discuss and to *want to* wrestle with issues long enough to really feel their significance. Tom wanted to go hit something or shoot something or bounce something. I wanted him to be a girl—and he wanted to be a guy. Imagine that! I experience victory over my Enemy when I let Tom be my husband and my "guy-friend" and when I let my girlfriends be . . . my girlfriends.

3. *MY GIRLFRIENDS ARE GREAT ACCOUNTABILITY PARTNERS—AND IT IS GOOD TO BE HELD ACCOUNTABLE*

Since each of us will one day give an account to God (Romans 14:12), it is good to practice for that day by giving an account to one another. I have another girlfriend who is my walking partner. Kathleen and I meet at 7:30 a.m. most weekday mornings to wear out the hill at Thompson Station Park. Since I've been in crisis mode all summer, poor Kathleen has put in up to six miles a day. I love Kathleen for walking with me. But I love her more for the way she listens without condemnation, then subtly offers scriptural wisdom. She is truly an accountability partner for me.

Be sure to remember that in order to have accountability partners you must be humble enough to listen when what you hear might not be what you want to hear. Be careful not to let your feelings dictate your willingness to grow and change.

4. IRON SHARPENS IRON AND FRIENDS SHARPEN FRIENDS

Even though I have not already attained the prize of my upward calling—this I know, I am pressing on (Philippians 3:12–14)! And my girlfriends encourage me along the way. When we set out to change the world, we simply do it better together!

Too many women live lonely lives. They isolate themselves and try to maintain the facade that all is well when all is not. We're so afraid that someone will find out our lives aren't perfect that we never let others close enough to experience genuine, God-honoring friendships. The Enemy defeats us by isolating us from the troops. When women are willing to share their lives with one another, they become a mighty army of valiant warriors. They disarm the Enemy when he comes against their marriages, their children, their health, and their homes. Don't miss out on anything God has for you by being afraid to develop deep friendships with other women.

WHAT'S NECESSARY FOR HEALTHY FRIENDSHIPS?

CONFIDENTIALITY

There are several things necessary for God-honoring, battle-winning friendships. The first is confidentiality. This is a rare treasure—to find someone who can keep her tongue tame. We women are notorious for sharing secrets with others in the name of "prayer requests." Be careful not to baptize gossip. Scripture lumps the wagging tongue in the same category as sexual immorality and idolatry.

> Put to death, therefore, whatever belongs to your earthly nature: sexual immorality, impurity, lust, evil desires and greed, which is idolatry. Because of these, the wrath of God is coming. You used to walk in these ways, in the life you once lived. But now you must rid yourselves of all such things as these: anger, rage, malice, *slander, and filthy language from your lips. Do not lie to each other,* since you have taken off your old self with its practices and have put on the new self, which is being renewed in knowledge in the image of its Creator.
>
> Colossians 3:5–10

Be a friend who keeps confidences, and look for women who can do the same.

But here's a warning: Confidentiality with your friends does not give you license to compromise the sacred trust you and your husband share. This is where many women open the door wide and compromise their marriage vows. There are some intimate matters that are sacred to your marriage. If you desecrate that intimacy, the Adversary will take full advantage of you.

- Don't discuss private matters that concern you and your husband with your friends. Let me qualify this by encouraging you to be careful to guard your husband's confidence and his trust. However, if your husband is involved in pornography, substance abuse, violent behavior, or other harmful activities, I encourage you to confide in godly friends and seek help for both you and your husband.
- Don't criticize your husband—even to blow off steam. Don't talk about anything that would cause your friend to think less of him. Why would you want to do that? You can do this with God when you pray.
- Don't talk about your sex life. That is a personal and intimate gift that belongs only to you and your husband.

INTEGRITY

Another virtue important to healthy friendship is integrity. Even though you may want to be friends with someone who can keep your secret safe, this is not license to speak freely about anything and everything—or to run rampant in the wrong direction. Good friends help each other stay on track with God's personal development plan. That plan is to create the image of Christ in you. One way you can do this is by maintaining integrity in your friendships.

> Finally [sisters], whatever is true, whatever is noble, whatever is right, whatever is pure, whatever is lovely, whatever is admirable—if anything is excellent or praiseworthy—think about such things.
>
> Philippians 4:8

LAUGHTER

This is *absolutely* necessary in friendships. You have got to find a friend who makes you laugh. Sure you'll cry sometimes, but laughter is good for the soul! There have been times when I've had to confess that if I had no sense of humor I'd have no sense at all.

When I laugh I am reminded that God is still on His throne, and He's still got my best interest at heart. I laugh to keep from taking myself and my circumstances too seriously. If you look hard enough you can find something to laugh about even in your depths of despair. Look for girlfriends who love to laugh with you. And find activities to do together that give you something to laugh about.

FORGIVENESS

You won't have a really good friend, and your friendship won't last for long, if you are not willing to forgive one another. Don't go into relationships thinking that you will never have disagreements or misunderstandings. If you dare to love your friends deeply, something is bound to go wrong. Go into your relationships with other women understanding that when something goes wrong, you will be tenderhearted and willing to forgive. "Be kind and compassionate to one another, forgiving each other, just as in Christ God forgave you" (Ephesians 4:32).

I just finished watching a series of movies based on the stories written by Lucy Maud Montgomery, tracing the fictional life of Anne of Green Gables. And as I watched that little orphan girl grow to be a beautiful woman, I was amazed at the many times she found herself in the middle of a conflict. Sometimes she got herself in trouble and at other times her trouble resulted from misunderstandings that grew out of a prejudice against orphans. As I watched Anne overcome these obstacles, I realized why so many women lack genuine, God-honoring friendships with other women.

The Enemy uses us to hurt one another, then coaxes us into a determination to harbor offense. Rather than develop the art of offering sincere apologies, we nurse grudges. The devil also taps into our flesh, stirring up our own insecurities and selfishness so that we focus our energy on self-preservation at all cost. But the price tag of preserving self is loneliness, and rather than preserve ourselves we lose ourselves in isolation from others.

Anne showed me how to overcome these attacks. She conquered her fear of confrontation, risked being honest, and did this over and over again, clothing herself in humility. Because of her efforts she broke through the crusty outer shells of her "Aunt" Marilla; Marilla's nosy neighbor Rachel Lind; Mrs. Barry, her best friend Diana's mother; as well as Diana's mean Aunt Jo. Later on Anne endeared herself to bitter, selfish old Mrs. Harris and prickly Katherine with a K. Anne sincerely loved people and tried her very best to be at peace with them all. Except for the prideful grudge that she insisted on carrying toward Gilbert Blythe, Anne never held grudges against anyone. And even that grudge against Gilbert was eventually released when Anne realized she loved him.

We would do well to learn from Anne of Green Gables. As I've embraced my own need for girlfriends, I've learned that the best way to win the battle for friends is to learn how to say seven powerful words:

"I am sorry. Will you forgive me?"

Several years ago the wife of one of our pastors disappointed me. While I might have been justified in my hurt over her letting me down, I certainly was not prepared for the spiritual warfare that erupted. She got angry right back at me. We were harsh with each other, and having been in the ministry for a very long time, I *knew* that this brokenness in our relationship could not bring any glory to God. But I was justified! She did let me down. And her wrongdoing would result in something not happening for our women. (I can't remember what that "something" was, but I'm sure it was significant.) I tried to have my quiet time, and I tried to tell God how sorry I was that she was so wrong. But God would have none of that. He reminded me that I'd been a believer since my childhood and she'd only come to know Him as an adult. He basically chastised me like He did Martha when she was so certain He'd reprimand Mary instead (see Luke 10:41–42). God clearly told me that I needed to take the high road.

When my children were young, I tried to teach them the power of taking the high road. Often they would encourage the other to take that road. One of them told me that she was perfectly happy to be on the low road. And if the truth be known, when this pastor's wife and I were at odds with each other, I was perfectly happy to be on the low road too. But God convicted my heart and told me that I needed to take her some humble pie. I am not a very good cook, so I went to the grocery, chose a pie from the freezer section, and took it with me to her house.

When she came to the door, her arms were crossed and her face was stern. She didn't seem that happy to see me—with or without my pie. But I pressed through despite my pounding heart and offered her my frozen pie with these words: "I want to give you a humble pie. I'm sincerely sorry for being so hard on you. Will you forgive me?"

She took my pie, wrapped me in a two-arm hug, and both of us cried. We ate a slice of pie together and have remained friends (close friends) from that day until this. I won that battle by eating humble pie. And although she and I didn't know it, there were hundreds of—maybe even a thousand—souls hanging in the balance of our choosing to overcome the brokenness in our relationship. Our church has added over a thousand people since that time, and her husband and mine have been able to work together without a cloud of conflict hovering over their wives.

Sometimes our friendships are there to teach us the lesson Jesus embraced on the cross. Friends teach us the importance of offering and receiving forgiveness. Neil Anderson teaches in his "7 Steps to Freedom" that forgiveness is not forgetting but rather a decision of your will to live with the consequences of another person's sin.[1]

HOW TO CREATE AND GROW HEALTHY FRIENDSHIPS WITH OTHER WOMEN

TAKE THE INITIATIVE!

Don't sit around and wait for someone to initiate a relationship with you; go out and choose someone you'd like to get to know better. Invite her for coffee, ice cream, lunch, or a poolside chat. What you do together isn't as important as getting together.

A few years ago I hosted my own birthday party. I was inspired by my children. For years I'd hosted their parties. We invited their friends to come, served them cake, played games, sent them home with goodie bags, and enjoyed the entire ordeal. Why should they have all the fun? A few weeks before my birthday I sent out invitations, then enlisted a caterer who prepared chicken salad (served on calorie-laden croissants) and cupcakes. I set up a pedicure/manicure parlor by pulling out my daughter's foot-washing tub. And I looked forward to entertaining my guests. We had a blast! And we ate adult cupcakes. There were no cupcakes with white frosting and sprinkles; we ate chocolate chunk cupcakes with mocha buttercream frosting, red velvet cupcakes with cream cheese frosting, and my personal favorite, strawberry cupcakes with strawberry cream frosting—I'm talking "adult only" cupcakes!

When I am looking for ideas of things to do with my friends, I am constantly inspired by my daughter Kaleigh. She and her friends come up with the best outings. We took three girlfriends and their moms to the mountains last winter and played one of those games where you have to think quick (thankfully we played in mother-daughter teams and Kaleigh is a genius!). Kaleigh goes to downtown Franklin (our picturesque little town) and buys nothing but a single-scoop ice-cream cone from Ben and Jerry's. At other times she and her friends go to the park and fly kites. Yesterday she went rock climbing! Your outings don't have to be that adventuresome! You could even have a firefly-catching contest and serve watermelon. The list is endless.

ALWAYS RETURN PHONE CALLS AND/OR E-MAILS

When someone calls you—call her back! This is not only a simple courtesy but also a friendship developer. The devil works overtime on our imaginations, and when you don't return her phone call, your friend might think you are mad at her or you don't like her or that she isn't important to you. What thoughts run through your mind when people don't return your phone calls or e-mails?

Initiate an old-fashioned phone call. Call another woman just to chat. Show genuine interest in what's going on in her life. When my parents built their dream home, they included a phone booth in the upstairs hallway. I spent many hours in that booth talking to my friends. Unfortunately, our children don't talk anymore. They communicate with one another; they just don't use their vocal chords. Facebook is fun, but to hear a warm voice in my ear is much more relational and much more likely to develop genuine friendships. I still smile today when I remember my grandmother getting on the "party line" at 7:00 p.m. each evening and talking with three or four of her friends.

REMEMBER SPECIAL DATES

Celebrate your girlfriends' anniversaries and birthdays (and the birthdays of her kids) and acknowledge the day her mother died, etc. Mark your calendar with her special dates. This simple act of thoughtfulness will build a bond of love that strengthens a powerful defense against the Enemy.

WHO ARE YOUR FRIENDS?

Stuart Briscoe wrote,

> The stuff of which spiritual life is made is communion with Christ and with people who share a heart for God, building up the things we have in common. David, at the hour of his greatest need, found divine provision in the prince who took the initiative of commitment and communion and ministered to him. Our Lord Jesus has demonstrated the same thing to us. What He asks us is, "In what way are we responding to Him and taking initiatives for befriending others?" I urge you, be one of God's answers in terms of fellowship and friendship with other people.[2]

You are missing much of God's provision for you if you are isolating yourself from others. It is important to have girlfriends of all shapes and sizes, all different ages, in different stages of life—and at varying levels of relationship. You will most likely have fewer friends at the deeper levels of friendship—because deep levels of relationship require time and emotional energy to sustain.

Consider your friends: Who are your casual friends? These are the women you would enjoy sitting with at ball games or the park—women you might eat Wednesday night supper with, or talk with for more than a passing moment in the halls at the church. You may have many casual friends. This might be the place where you'll find a closer friend.

Who are your trustworthy friends? These are women you know you could count on in the time of need. Perhaps they are your neighbors—though you hardly ever see them, you'd feel perfectly comfortable asking them to feed the dog and fetch the mail while you're out of town. You may even call them if you got in a pinch and needed an egg for your brownies or someone to watch your baby for a quick errand.

Who are your confidants? These are friends that you've spent time really talking with. You may talk with her every day—you may not! But when you talk, you go well below the surface and get to the nitty gritty. This is a friend who knows your crazy sister, and knows exactly how you feel—because she has a crazy sister too. She's the one you wish you could spend more time with.

Who is your "kindred spirit"? By kindred, I'm talking about Jonathan and David kind of friendships. This is your BFF! The shoulder you go to cry on. This is the one who is always ready to take off to the mountains or to the beach—or to the hospital when a loved one's had a wreck. She's the one you eat ice cream and chocolate with—and the same one you weigh in with at Weight Watchers not knowing *why* those scales don't cooperate!

Blessed are you if you have friends in each of these categories! I hope you realize that you need healthy friendships, and that God will honor these relationships as He works in them to bring glory to himself.

Satan Targets My Friendships With Other Women

Is there a friend you need to forgive? Perhaps there is more than one. If so, I want you to jot their names in the space provided.

Pray this prayer over each person until you have honestly decided to let them go.

Lord, I choose to forgive________________________ (name the person or people) for (what they did) because it made me feel (how you felt). Lord, I choose not to hold on to my resentment. I thank you for setting me free from the bondage of my bitterness. I relinquish my right to seek revenge and ask you to heal my damaged emotions. I now ask you to bless those who have hurt me. In Jesus' name I pray. Amen.

ADAPTED FROM NEIL ANDERSON'S "STEPS TO FREEDOM IN CHRIST"[3]

Is there a friend you cherish? Consider calling her right now and scheduling a coffee date. Tell her how much she means to you.

Pray this prayer:

Thank you, Lord, for the women in my life. Please proclaim your name through the way we love one another. Help me to be an encouragement to my friends. Help me to love them the way you want to love them. I want to be your hands and your feet in their lives. Help me to overcome my fears and insecurities so that I can develop true friends. Help me to lay aside pride and offense so that I can keep the true friends you give me. Be glorified in my friendships so the Enemy will flee.

SHARPEN YOUR SWORD

When we love one another we testify of God. 1 John 4:12

To love the Lord and to love one another are the greatest commands. Matthew 22:37–40

God comforts us so that we can comfort others. 2 Corinthians 1:3–4

Whatever! Philippians 4:8

Your friendships with others will require forgiveness. Ephesians 4:32

Commit the Word to memory: A friend will also make a great Scripture memory partner. Choose a verse to memorize together and recite it aloud as you walk or sip coffee together.

Chapter Ten

Satan Targets My Health

> Lord, you have assigned me my portion and my cup; you have made my lot secure. The boundary lines have fallen for me in pleasant places; surely I have a delightful inheritance. I will praise the Lord, who counsels me, even at night my heart instructs me. I have set the Lord always before me. Because he is at my right hand, I will not be shaken.
>
> Psalm 16:5–8

THE SPIRITUAL NATURE OF SICKNESS

I am convinced that all illness and injury are rooted in sin. However, not all sickness is directly related to specific sin in someone's life (see John 9:2–3). Because we live in a sin-stained world, we are subject to physical suffering and eventual death. God explained this to Adam and Eve when He met them after they ate the forbidden fruit. (Read Genesis 3.) Ever since Adam and Eve were expelled from the garden of Eden, people have suffered and died as a result of sin. Scripture says, "There is a time for everything, and a season for every activity under heaven: a time to be born and a time to die" (Ecclesiastes 3:1–2).

However, there are times when the Enemy uses disease and disasters not only to inflict pain in God's children but also to distract them from proclaiming God's name to the world. At those times the battle becomes personal and our response becomes powerful. In this chapter I will share some excerpts from the thoughts I recorded when I first discovered my own cancer. I will also share an excerpt from the journal of my friend Jenny who died of cancer.

I don't have the space in this chapter, nor the knowledge, to deal with arthritis, paralysis, leukemia, psoriasis, or all the other millions of things that can go wrong with our bodies. I chose cancer because it is common and I have personal experience with it. My prayer is that as you read Jenny's and my thoughts, which we recorded while we were fighting our battles, you will be encouraged to win the battles that wage against your health and the health of those you love.

FROM MY JOURNAL

MONDAY, MARCH 1

Wow, how do I even begin to describe today? Last night I was choking down the laxative to prepare for the colonoscopy, and when I awoke after the procedure, I was thrilled that we were done. Honestly, I thought we'd get out of that office and celebrate God's goodness to us—eat a Cracker Barrel breakfast and thank God for being so gracious and kind. When Dr. Caudill sat on the bed and said, "We've got a problem," my world stopped spinning. As he described the "most likely cancerous growth" he found in me, I cried—I was shaking and cold. I watched Tom take it in, calm as a cucumber . . . and I saw my calendar: Vegas this weekend, Mikel's eighteenth birthday next weekend, Florida the next weekend, then our exciting, crazy trip to Ethiopia to visit the orphans. . . . Suddenly the dates went blank.

Tom didn't go to Hattie Hill as he planned. [Hattie Hill is what we call our happy place in the North Carolina mountains.] He sat with me the entire day and assured me we were doing this together. All I could respond with was, "I am so sorry." And I am!

I'm sure I'm not going to Ethiopia; I don't know about Vegas and Florida. I don't know anything except I have a very sick colon. Weird kind of sickness—silent and little-known. We go back to Dr. Caudill's office tomorrow for him to refer us to a cancer doctor and a surgeon. The mass has to come out. And most likely if it is indeed cancer there will be radiation and chemotherapy. I've heard all about these things—but always when I was ministering to someone else.

Lots of thoughts have run through my head today. I've shaken and cried; I've taken small naps. Tom and I have held each other and talked about our fiftieth wedding anniversary—about how I'll be pushing him around in his wheelchair while he drools. I've seen my daughters' weddings like movies in my mind and hoped I would live to see TJ graduate from high school. Our little old dog, Halo, has actually been a comfort to me today. There's been something very consoling about hearing him sleep in the room where I am. And I've wondered if I'll outlive him.

We haven't told the kids yet. Mikel drilled me with questions tonight while she was driving home. And Kaleigh asked how my test went. I told Kaleigh everything was fine and I told Mikel that I would know more tomorrow when we talk to the doctor. TJ didn't ask. They are all enjoying their worlds just like I was enjoying mine—we have to tell them tomorrow.

That's what I dread most—telling them, my parents, and our family. I actually don't mind telling the church. And I am eager to tell my prayer partners. I so need them to come alongside me in this. God knew I would. The only thing I don't like about the "world" knowing is the outpouring of ministry directed toward me. It's just a lot to handle right now.

Grace-filled. That's how I want to walk through this . . . filled with grace.

I don't know what this means for this week, much less next month. I don't know whether to cancel my speaking engagements or to plan to fulfill them. I don't know if I need to be cherishing the moments or believing I'll live forever—like I guess I was thinking before Dr. Caudill sat on my bed.

Verses that have ministered to me today are Romans 8:28, Philippians 4:6–7, and James 4:8.

God is good. He's just as good today as He was yesterday and the day before. He's just as good as He will be tomorrow and the day after that. He promises to be with me, to give me power, and to fill me with peace. I promise to trust Him, to place my life in the palm of His hands, and to be a living sacrifice.

You are good, Lord. And you are Lord. You have given me so much—more than most. You have filled my life with abundance. My cup overflows. The boundary lines have fallen to me in pleasant places; my lot is secure. Where you lead I'll go. I trust you. Amen.

TUESDAY, MARCH 2

A day seems like a year. I'm better tonight than I was last night. We've begun the process of telling people. It snowed this morning (but didn't stick). I told Tom that these were two of the ugliest days I've ever seen and that I liked it that way. I figure if my world is caving in there is a small measure of solace in the fact that everyone else is cold and gloomy with me.

We went back to Dr. Caudill's office today. Ruby gave me a little silver angel thing. She put it in my hand and hugged me. It was so sweet; to think that we've known her and David (and their son Justin) for twenty-one years. David was the first person to ever accept Christ when we came to Thompson Station!! How wonderful that God would see fit to place Ruby in Dr. Caudill's office for such a time as this. There was a supernatural sense of comfort when she wrapped her arms around me. Kind of like being assured that twenty-one years of ministry is right here to walk with me through this.

Then Dr. Caudill explained what we do and don't know. The pathology report confirmed cancer. Next we do blood work to check the liver and I'm not sure what else, and then we go to get a CT scan (tomorrow), then to meet the radiation doctor (Thursday) and a surgeon (a former kicker for some professional football team—Monday). He told me I could still go to Vegas this weekend—if I was mentally and emotionally up to it. I am. But Florida might need to be put on hold. Then he prayed with us. It was a very sweet prayer—trusting us all to God, asking Him to heal me—and praying for the other doctors who would be part of the plan. It was enlightening to hear a doctor pray for other doctors. He thanked God for making him one, and asked God to give him wisdom. He thanked God for the skills and abilities of the others and asked that they would be on their "A game" when they came to me.

Tom told him I was teaching on spiritual warfare at church right now, and Dr. Caudill asked us if we thought this was spiritual warfare. I told him I didn't know but that if it was, my body is the temple of the Holy Spirit. And if the Enemy wants to attack the temple then whatever he sends in is now under the sovereign authority of God because His Spirit rules His house. God told me that this morning.

Dr. Caudill liked that answer. Then he gave me a prayer (on a prescription pad). This is what it said: "Teach me what I need to be taught. Take me where I need to be taken, and use me how I need to be used."

He said it was a dangerous prayer.

Yeah . . . but who else do I trust? If not God, who?! He's the Lover of my Soul and the Keeper of my life! Lord, you are trustworthy.

This morning I asked God what He wanted of me. He told me He wanted what He's always wanted: complete dependence, trust, and obedience.

I can do that.

I was sick all day over the dread of having to tell our kids. Ruby brought us dinner (from Cracker Barrel, where I thought I was having breakfast yesterday). And we gathered everyone around. They already knew something was up. Tom went into so much detail (about my cancer) we all got tickled—only as the sweetness of God could allow this incredible family He's given me. They were all three sobered. They begged Dad to stop with the gory details, and they cried a bit. TJ said that if the Mayans were right we all only have three years before the end of the world comes anyway (something about their calendars ending in 2012). Then he told Mikel and Kaleigh that in fifty years this doesn't matter at all—it's just a timing thing. Kaleigh cried a bit, assured me that she loved me, and reminded me that she's God's favorite and that I would win this battle because God's favor on her would overflow on me. I said I'd accept that gladly.

Mikel already had an inkling that something was wrong. She cried some, and sat with me after everyone else was gone. She read aloud the essays she's working on for school and cried over the one she wrote about her best friend, Halo. Very sweet. She reminded me that her homeroom prays every day and they would be praying for me. She also reminded us all that Barb had this same cancer and is doing great. Thank you, Lord, for that reminder!!

Those kids are amazing, Lord. Simply amazing. You are so good to me to give me these incredible children.

The GLORY has begun!

Thank you, Lord, that your Word is true. I praise you because you are God and because you are good. I love you—as much now as ever. And I trust you completely.

SPIRITUAL WARFARE IN MY BODY

When Dr. Caudill asked Tom and me if we thought my cancer was spiritual warfare, I didn't really know. Was it a coincidence that I started teaching on spiritual warfare just a month before my cancer was diagnosed? Is *all* cancer spiritual warfare? I honestly don't know. As I said in the introduction to this chapter, I'm convinced that all disease and all disaster have sin at their root. They were not part of God's original design—and they are part of the suffering He sent Jesus to save us from.

I do know that God's Word promises that we will one day live in a new heaven and a new earth; and that in that new place there will be no more cancer, no more muscular dystrophy, no more birth defects, car accidents, or amputations (Revelation 21:1–5).

But until that day comes, the physical pain and suffering we bear can either be used to proclaim or profane the name of the Lord. Therefore, the Enemy is lurking in the crevices of our physical well-being and looking for a way to gain some ground in his battle against the glory of God.

My response to Dr. Caudill came out of a sincere conviction that God has plans for my life. I've clung to Jeremiah 29:11 as my life verse for many years. My response to him also came from a solid understanding of the way God hems me in. I agree with David when he wrote Psalm 16. God has assigned me my portion and my cup (Psalm 16:5). Because I've invited Jesus to be my Lord, and because I seek to obey His Word, He orders my steps. That means that He assigns me my portion and my cup.

Because I've dedicated my life to God, God himself determines what is allowed in and out of my life. He grants permission when the Enemy is allowed to harm me. God numbers my days and tells me what He wants me to do with them. If I am diagnosed with

My Portion and My Cup

When David penned Psalm 16, he was referencing God's purposes and plans for his life. David's portion was not only the amount of blessings God saw fit to give him but also the frequency and severity of trials and disappointments. David's cup referred to the assignments God had for David to complete. David's statement is a profession of contentment and submission, of trust and confidence. Jesus mentioned God's cup when He prayed in the garden of Gethsemane. His too was a prayer of submission. (See Luke 22:42.)

cancer, then God has allowed cancer to be filtered through His plans for my life.

Job experienced suffering at the hands of Satan but at the permission of God (Job 1). Any suffering that comes my way has to come by the same route that it came to Job. When suffering attacks my body, I am more than certain that God will be glorified in it. For Scripture teaches me that my body is the temple of the Holy Spirit (1 Corinthians 3:16 and 6:19–20).

In the Old Testament the temple represented the dwelling place of God. It was a holy place. The priests ministered to the Lord by taking care of His temple. In the New Testament we learn that God no longer dwells in buildings but rather in people, more specifically in our bodies. We are the living, breathing, walking, talking temples of God! I'm not sure we grasp the significance of that. God longs to express himself (to make His name known) among the nations today. So rather than draw all people to a specific place, He sends His temple to them. We are the temple, the earthly dwelling place of God.

When our temples are sick, we can know that the sickness has entered a holy place. I found great comfort in this thought. Cancer was an enemy to me. It had invaded my body/temple. And although I didn't know what damage cancer had done, I did know *who* was in my temple. Therefore, I knew that cancer had to submit itself to God's authority and sovereign rule in my body.

I was reminded of what happened to Dagon, the Philistines' god—a carved idol that was half man and half fish. When the Philistines conquered the Israelites in a battle, they took the ark of God and placed it next to Dagon in his temple. (You can read this story in 1 Samuel 5:1–4.) On the first day the people came to the temple and found their god Dagon fallen on his face before the ark of God. They took their god and put him back in his place. On the next day Dagon was back on the ground facedown before the ark of God, only this time his head and hands had been broken off and were lying on the threshold.

My dear sister in Christ, if you have invited Jesus to live in your heart and to rule in your life, then your body is the temple of the Holy Spirit! If cancer or fibromyalgia, depression or heart disease, chicken pox or yellow fever invade your body, those things must bow down to the lordship of Christ. Either God will heal you of your disease and bring glory to himself or He will powerfully sustain you as you suffer and still bring glory to himself.

God healed me of cancer through the skill of my surgeon and other medical professionals. And He did it for His very own glory.

TWO DIFFERENT STORIES, ONE GREAT AND GLORIOUS LORD

But He allowed cancer to kill my young friend Jenny. Jenny's cancer was diagnosed in the first few months of her pregnancy. She and her husband chose to carry their baby even at the risk of her cancer spreading throughout the pregnancy. We prayed her cancer would not spread. When Gabriel was born, Jenny's cancer had spread. So Jenny began a long journey of chemo and radiation treatments. Finally she was declared cancer free. This is what she wrote to us:

> Hey, everyone! How do I begin? I just don't even know where to start. I know that most of you know that I had the CT scan over a week ago now, and you have been waiting for an e-mail to let you all know the results of that scan. Your wait is finally over. I have been waiting to tell everyone because it was really important to me that my church family hear it from me this morning and not through the grapevine. They have done so much for us, loving on us and taking care of us, and I felt like I owed that to them. I knew that I needed to do that so I kept it very quiet all week long. It was a long week! On Monday morning my doctor told me that my cancer is gone! Praise the Lord! He is so good and so faithful. This has been the hardest time in my life but so worth everything I have gone through. In the end, I have a beautiful, healthy baby boy and I get to stay here and be with all five of the blessings that God has given me, Joshua [Jenny's husband] included!
>
> I will never understand why God chose me to minister to so many people out of what has been the most painful experience of my life, but I sure am thankful He did. I have met so many people and become close friends with others through this trial in my life. I have seen the love of Christ in my church as they have given 110 percent to us at all times. I have been encouraged by cards, e-mails, letters, and phone calls for months. This experience has taught me so much about myself as a person. I never knew I could have the faith that God gave me. I never knew I could have the strength that only He could have given me. He is so good, all the time. I have never looked back. And I saw

> Him work so perfectly on my behalf. He has done so much more for me than I could even put into words. His Word is so true. When we trust in Him and acknowledge Him, He makes our path straight. He is so faithful and He loves us so much more than we know. I can't imagine my life without Him and can't understand why anyone would turn from Him after hearing just parts of my story. I have learned that God is in control and I trust Him completely. If the outcome had been bad, I would still feel the same way. He is good all the time, and I am so thankful for all of you who have prayed without ceasing for me and my family. I love you all and pray God's richest blessing on you all!
>
> Love and many blessings,
> Jenny Carlisle

Unfortunately Jenny's story was not yet finished. Her cancer returned and she died seven months later. Here is one more excerpt from her journal, written in December before she died in February.

> I am so tired and I am having a hard time not getting a little down. . . . The thoughts of this being my last Christmas are haunting me right now. They just remind me to go back to living every day like it could be my last. God wants us living that way anyway! None of us know when our last moment on earth will be, so we have to live every moment to the fullest. That is what I have decided to do. I am also not going to be afraid to tell those I love how I feel and what I think. If God lays it on my heart to speak with someone about Him, I am not going to be quiet. Jesus could come back today and those we love could be left behind because we didn't take the opportunity to tell people about Him. What better time of year to share Jesus than the time of His birth? I challenge all of us to tell someone about Him this holiday season.

I love you all, and I am so thankful for all your love, prayers, and support throughout this very long journey.

Love and blessings,
Jenny Carlisle

The night Jenny died I was privileged to be part of the circle of loved ones in her bedroom. She had an index card taped to the wall just above her bed. And on the index card Romans 15:13 was printed in my handwriting. God gave me this verse as His Word to pray over Jenny. She was so young, the mother of four small children, and always faithful to praise God every step of her painful journey with cancer. I didn't have a clue why she had to die. But as we sang hymns and enjoyed the peaceful presence of God in that holy place, Jenny's mother made reference to the verse. She said, "Leighann, we thought this verse was for Jenny, but it was really for us—for us right now."

> May the God of hope fill you with all joy and peace as you trust in him, so that you may overflow with hope by the power of the Holy Spirit.

I want you to know that Jenny won the spiritual battle that waged against her that night just as I won the one that waged against me several weeks ago when Dr. Herline called to tell me my lymph nodes were cancer free. Jenny believed God and served Him faithfully as she fought with all her might to live. Because she never faltered in her faith, Jenny died testifying to the sovereignty and glory of God.

The Enemy will certainly enjoy messing with your mind when you wrestle with your health. But that is a battle you can win. Your body is a temple of God. Whatever invades your temple is at the mercy of God. If you find yourself fighting this battle today, trust God and obey His Word.

Satan Targets My Health

Underline 1 Corinthians 3:16 and 6:19 in your Bible.

Knowing God like you know Him today, would you be willing to pray Dr. Caudill's "dangerous prayer"?

Lord, teach me what I need to be taught, take me where I need to be taken, and use me how I need to be used.

SHARPEN YOUR SWORD

The Lord assigns you your portion. Psalm 16:5

Be anxious for nothing. Philippians 4:6–7

God is as near as you want Him to be. James 4:8

Your body is the temple of the Holy Spirit. 1 Corinthians 3:16 and 6:19–20

The God of hope will fill you with peace. Romans 15:13

Commit the Word to memory: I know many women who are homebound due to health issues. My friend Nancy crochets prayer shawls for others to use when they are going through difficult times. Many women I know whose activities are limited spend time with the Lord in His Word. If your activities are limited by your health, commit God's Word to memory. Create prayer cards, read them aloud for a solid week, then mail them to someone else who needs to be encouraged.

CHAPTER ELEVEN

Satan Targets My Church

The body is a unit, though it is made up of many parts; and though all its parts are many, they form one body. So it is with Christ.

1 CORINTHIANS 12:12

For over twenty years my speaking ministry has provided me with the opportunity to travel to countless churches. I've worshiped with churches in most of the United States and in Japan, Nicaragua, Germany, India, Mexico, the Bahamas, and China. And one thing I've discovered about God's church is that in each congregation she is more than what she could be and less than what she should be. By the grace of Jesus Christ we are growing toward completion, and God is intent on nurturing our growth. At the same time we have an Enemy chomping at our heels. He is just as interested in stunting our growth as God is in growing us up. Satan wants to render our witness null and void. He does this in several ways:

First, he blinds us to the truth of our relationship with Christ and the power that results from that relationship. Then he keeps us preoccupied with projects and theological debates. Third, he entices us to remain self-absorbed in order to keep us from experiencing the powerful force we might become when we lay down our lives for the sake of unity in the Body.

In this chapter I will expose the Enemy's attack against the church; then I will tell you how you can win the spiritual battle for your church. As women we have a unique role to play in God's church. It's been said that we're full of "sugar and spice and everything nice." God created us with the distinct ability to create an atmosphere of nurture and love in our churches—an atmosphere conducive to allowing God to cultivate growth in and through us. As you read this chapter ask yourself this question: What can I do to partner with God for the health of my church?

Don't forget that God loves His church. The church is His bride. He longs to present His bride to himself holy and pure. As we learn to love God's church the way He loves His church, we will be better able to accomplish God's purpose in our world today.

> Husbands, love your wives, just as Christ loved the church and gave himself up for her to make her holy, cleansing her by the washing with water through the word, and to present her to himself as a radiant church, without stain or wrinkle or any other blemish, but holy and blameless.
>
> EPHESIANS 5:25–27

STRATEGY NUMBER ONE: SATAN BLINDS BELIEVERS

I am convinced that the reason the devil is often successful in rendering God's church weak and powerless is because the saints forget who they are in Christ. Let's go back to 1 Samuel 17. When David arrived on the battlefield with his bread and cheese, he noticed something the entire Israelite army missed. It was a tiny, seemingly insignificant detail—completely overlooked in the Israelites' vivid description of their giant. But that one tiny, seemingly insignificant detail made all the difference in the world!

David saw Goliath's size, he heard Goliath shout, and then David watched as the entire Israelite army ran from their giant in fear. While the trained and experienced soldiers trembled in their tents, David asked a profound question:

> What will be done for the man who kills this Philistine and removes this disgrace from Israel? Who is this *uncircumcised Philistine* that he should defy the armies of the living God?
>
> 1 SAMUEL 17:26

David noticed something the rest of Israel's mighty army missed. Goliath was big; he wore impressive armor and carried a massive spear. But even dressed to the hilt, Goliath could not hide the fact that he was uncircumcised.

Now, when I was in the fifth grade girls' Sunday school class, I remember us putting Mrs. Lewis in the hot seat. We were studying some Old Testament story, and we were introduced to the word *circumcision*. Being the curious Bible students we were, we insisted Mrs. Lewis explain circumcision to us. After we pressed her relentlessly she said, "Well, it's a ceremony the Israelite men went through to express their covenant relationship with God."

Well, that didn't satisfy us at all. "Ceremony that expresses a covenant relationship with God" sounded to us like the teacher on the Peanuts television special that aired each October, "*Bla, bla, bla-bla-bla, bla.*" So we continued to ask, "What?! We want to know exactly what they did in this ceremony!"

Finally Mrs. Lewis explained circumcision in graphic detail. What else could she do? Once she finished with her explanation, her cheeks flared crimson along with ours. We humbly giggled and simply responded, "Oh!"

But here's the deal. God set the Israelites apart as His favored people. He chose to love them, pour His heart into them, and set them apart from all other nations. Their circumcision was a physical expression of this covenant relationship they had with God. The act of circumcision was instituted by God as a reminder of the difference between the Israelite men and the rest of the world. You can read all about God's idea and the covenant relationship circumcision represented in Genesis 17.

When David mentioned Goliath's uncircumcised status, he brought that giant down to size. Rather than make note of Goliath's size or the weight of his spear, David focused on the *fact* that Goliath was *not* a part of God's plan for Israel!

"Who is this uncircumcised Philistine who dares to defy the armies of the living God?"

With that in mind, David found himself in a riverbed carefully choosing five smooth stones. Because David understood that Goliath did not belong in Judah and because David knew the Israelite soldiers were not trained to tremble, David put his faith in action and God killed Goliath with a stone.

I mentioned before that I've written a book on this chapter in Samuel because I am encouraged by David's courage—but more so by God's power. And the way I see it, if God is the same yesterday, today, and forever, then watch out world! For there are women of God worshiping in His churches today who are ready to take some giants down!

The Enemy would have you believe that you are a mere mortal—weak, powerless, outsized, and outsmarted by the giants he puts in your path. But God's Word tells you that you are so much more. You have a covenant relationship with the Lord God Almighty. The same God who used David to take Goliath down with a slingshot and a stone is the same God who longs to make His glory known through your church today.

David took Goliath down—and the whole world discovered there was a God in Israel. My dear sister saint—you can take your giants down too. You see, we are women, not men, and although we are not circumcised by human hands, God has performed a circumcision of sorts on us as well.

> For in Christ all the fullness of the Deity lives in bodily form, and you have been given fullness in Christ, who is the head over every power and authority. In him you were also circumcised, in the putting off of the sinful nature, not with a circumcision done by the hands of men but with the circumcision done by Christ, having been buried with him in baptism and raised with him through your faith in the power of God, who raised him from the dead.
>
> COLOSSIANS 2:9–12

We live in a covenant relationship with God. When Jesus died on the cross, He severed us from sin. We have been buried with Christ and raised to live lives of faith *in the power of* God! Satan wants you to forget that fact. Because you are a daughter of the King, the giants that heckle you are not put there to destroy you. God's sovereignty allows those giants to intersect your life. You may want to ask, "Leighann, why on earth would God do that?" The answer to this honest question is important; therefore, I'm going to print it in **bold** type and *italicize* it:

> ***The giants God allows Satan to put in your life (as fierce and ferocious as they might seem) are divine invitations (filtered through the heart of God) for you to partner with God in taking them down so the world will know there is a God in your corner of it.***

God longs to make His power known through your life and through your church. Remember who you are *in Christ*. Keep reading—chapter 12 deals with this subject more.

STRATEGY NUMBER TWO: SATAN KEEPS BELIEVERS BUSY

I can walk into any church this coming Sunday and be overwhelmed by the activities they are engaged in. Churches host fish-fry dinners, prayer meetings, women's Bible studies, quilting classes, vacation Bible school, men's beast feasts, and countless other activities. But the culture surrounding the church remains largely unchanged. Homosexuality is considered a choice to be protected and abortion is still legal. Why are our churches dying while our lostness is thriving?

The Enemy is not the least bit threatened by your fellowship suppers and your scrapbooking parties. In fact, he likes all that! Just so long as you don't develop real relationships with one another and just so you don't take your relationship with God too seriously.

Another tactic he uses to keep the church busy is to distract the saints when they do get together to study God's Word. If Satan can entice them to drown in discussions of predestination and premillenialism, he doesn't have to worry about them taking seriously Jesus' command for us to love our neighbors as ourselves. While saints huddle in their homes searching the Internet for more proof of their theological positions, they will not be outside striking up conversations with their lost friends next door.

Then, if by chance one of those lost friends happens to give their church a try even without a personal invitation, all the devil has to do is get Sally Sue sideways with Millie May as they discuss TULIP Calvinism in Sunday school. Ta-da! The neighbor goes home disillusioned, having never heard two women say such terrible things to each other, not even in the PTA meetings.

The Enemy attacks the church with busyness and distractions. He encourages those gathered together to put the emPHAsis on the wrong sylLAble, and in doing so he keeps God's powerful army lulled to sleep while the culture around them goes to hell.

STRATEGY NUMBER THREE: SATAN KEEPS BELIEVERS SELFISH

Satan doesn't have to work too hard on this particular strategy, for selfishness comes naturally to most people (even those whose lives have been redeemed). Paul urged the Corinthians to beware of this strategy the Enemy uses against the church. He encouraged the Corinthian believers to realize that they were individually vital to the church, but that together they were unstoppable (1 Corinthians 12:12–31). We forget this truth today. Too many people attend church for themselves and for themselves only. They come looking for what they can take home with them—rather than looking for how they can give themselves away. Most Sunday "go to meeting" people want to feel good when they worship, be entertained by the sermon, be fed in their classes, and be able to drive away quickly when they leave.

I have to confess that I sit in church staff meetings weekly where we spend hours discussing how we can meet these expectations. Is our worship as great as it could be? Do our sermons meet the people where they are? Is there more we can do to train our teachers so that their classes are fulfilling? And what can we do about parking? These are all legitimate concerns for church leaders. But if we are driven by these concerns, are we tempted to fall in the trap of cultivating selfish people? How does the "What can I get from this?" mentality line up with Jesus' call to real discipleship in Luke 9:23, "If anyone would come after me, he must *deny himself* and take up his cross daily and follow me"?

Self-centered people cannot be united with one another. Selfishness cripples the church because self-centered people remain divided. The church is most powerful when it is united in heart and mind: one spirit, one mind, one heart, one mission. Jesus' heart cry before He left us was that we would live in oneness with one another:

> My prayer is not for them alone. I pray also for those who will believe in me through their message, that all of them may be one, Father, just as you are in me and I am in you. May they also be in us so that the world may believe that you have sent me. I have given them the glory that you gave me, that they may be one as we are one: I in them and you in me. May they be brought to complete unity to let the world know that you sent me and have loved them even as you have loved me.
>
> JOHN 17:20–23

If you are an active member of a church, you know how hard the Enemy works against the unity of the saints. I've seen him succeed over the silliest things: color of the carpet, the location of a piano, the cost of a door, who's going to mow the grass, the list could go on and on. If the Enemy can keep believers selfish, and if he can persuade them to argue with one another, they will be so busy fighting the battles within that they will have neither the energy nor the motivation to fight the battles God invites them to win.

This is perhaps the most effective strategy Satan unleashes against God's church because it is the most difficult to overcome. In order to win the battle of selfishness we must . . . kill the flesh. Dying to self is hard, but it is also a necessary component of being a disciple of Christ. The words of Jesus concerning true discipleship are worth repeating here:

> If anyone would come after me, he must deny himself and take up his cross daily and follow me. For whoever wants to save his life will lose it, but whoever loses his life for me will save it.
>
> LUKE 9:23–24

HOW TO WIN THE BATTLE AT CHURCH

Most of the battles I've seen waged in church have had key players that were women. By nature we tend to get in the middle of things, motivated by the sincere conviction that we can fix it. In my first skirmish God showed me a powerful truth. We were fighting a spiritual battle in our church that was intense. Unfortunately, it felt intensely personal to me since my husband seemed to be the target of attack. I referenced this particular battle earlier in this book. What I learned (the hard way) was that the more I tried to talk and reason with people, the more I created a mess. I thought that I could just proclaim truth to the women who were confused and that through my proclamation of truth I would win this thing!

I underestimated the evil intent of the Enemy and overestimated my ability to talk my way out of the battle. I went over to different people's houses and sipped coffee at their kitchen tables. I tried to love on them and reason with them and tell them all about my husband's heart. But after I went home, they took my own words, added their tainted perceptions to them, then spread them like poison all over two counties. It was as if my efforts to talk us out of trouble fueled the flames of deception!

Finally, God showed me Exodus 14:14, "The Lord will fight for you while you keep silent" (NASB).

Keeping silent wasn't something I was good at. It was hard, but in matters of spiritual warfare, truth alone does not remedy the situation. Truth tends to be relative, and feelings, preconceived notions, falsehoods, and deceptions rule the day. Until God's Holy Spirit reveals truth to His people, we can talk until we are blue in the face and the devil will twist our words and use them like Tom's "waconda juice" (a mixture of oil and gasoline that he uses to light our campfires) to fuel the dissension.

For me to "keep silent" I had to trust God. I'm going to talk about this more in the next part of this book; but for now just know that trusting God is the single most significant thing you can do in warfare. For when the powers of darkness unleash their attack on you (or your church), their strength lies in the deception that

God can't be trusted. God is trustworthy! And trusting God will defeat the Enemy every time.

> Trust in the Lord with all your heart and lean not on your own understanding; in all your ways acknowledge him, and he will make your paths straight.
>
> PROVERBS 3:5–6

BE SIGNIFICANT

A few years ago I taught a conference titled "How to Lead a Significant Ministry." I took my key points from an article I'd read that was written by Tim Bowman, who was quoting Dr. Bingham Hunter of Trinity Evangelical Divinity School.[1] According to Dr. Hunter, God determines significance in these three ways:

1. **Obedience is significant**
2. **Humility is significant**
3. **Servanthood is significant**

If we determine to walk in obedience to God, in humility with one another, and as sincere servants to His kingdom, we will win the battle that wages against God's church. Let me briefly discuss each of these.

OBEDIENCE IS SIGNIFICANT

The first measure of greatness is obedience. When Jesus delivered His Sermon on the Mount He said this about greatness:

> Anyone who breaks one of the least of these commandments and teaches others to do the same will be called least in the kingdom of heaven, but whoever practices and teaches these commands will be called great in the kingdom of heaven.
>
> MATTHEW 5:19

Consider your obedience to God. Is it easier to teach on prayer—or to pray? Do you find it more entertaining to tell others how to connect with their neighbors than for you to connect with yours? Isn't it easier to fill in the blanks in your Bible study notebooks than it is to be patient with your teenager when she flaunts her attitude in your face and dares you to disagree with her? And even *if* the other women in your Bible study group think you're doing a great job, and the people sitting next to you on Sunday morning think you sing like an angel—God knows that you bit her sassy head off and nearly tossed it into kingdom come!

Are you obedient in how you live your priorities? If your greatest critic bugged your home, would she fall asleep listening to the recording? Or would she be energized with fuel for a bonfire? Does your life reflect what you say you believe?

Personal obedience to God is not only good—it is critical in winning spiritual battles.

HUMILITY IS SIGNIFICANT

> At that time the disciples came to Jesus and asked, "Who is the greatest in the kingdom of heaven?" He called a little child and had him stand among them. And he said: "I tell you the truth, unless you change and become like little children, you will never enter the kingdom of heaven. Therefore, whoever humbles himself like this child is the greatest in the kingdom of heaven."
>
> MATTHEW 18:1–4

Bowman shared that he remembered these three "counterweights" to assist him in keeping proper perspective:

- God's grace
- my fallibility
- the indispensability of others

Ask yourself, "Where would I be today without God's salvation?"

Most of the time my own humility is most threatened when other staff members come along who don't know what I've gone through and what I've done along the way. I find myself wanting to remind them! I do this when we pray at staff meetings. "Lord, thank you for being faithful to me, when there were only three Sunday school teachers and I recruited four more. Look at us now, Lord—oh, how it hurt when forty of them left and you brought a hundred more!" Am I rejoicing in what only God can do, or stroking my fragile ego in making sure men and women who serve with me are reminded of my willingness to do the hard work while they were enjoying some large church somewhere else (or growing up!)?

For some of you, humility might most often be threatened in affirmation. "Oh, Theresa! That was an incredible study on Philippians! I've never considered those insights before! Girl, you've got a gift!" And then Theresa might respond with something like this: "Thank you. I study, I mean for hours! And at about midnight-thirty, God shows up and tells me things I would not know!" Are you praising God or playing tug of war with His glory?

A great way to remain humble is to remember that you are fallible. This isn't hard for me—God has ways of reminding me just in case I forget. Either we will humble ourselves—or God will do the honors: "Humble yourselves therefore under the mighty hand of God, that he may exalt you in due time" (1 Peter 5:6 KJV).

Recognizing our own fallibility ought to lead us toward compassion and gentleness when dealing with the shortcomings of others as well.

And third, remember that no one person carries her own ministry. Realize the indispensable impact of others. For me this includes a look back: Who led me to the Lord? Who taught the four-year-olds on Sunday nights at First Baptist Church Atlanta so that I had a place to learn while my parents were in their classes? Who transformed an old laundry annex building into a biblical village for VBS when

I was six? Who gave the money to pay for scholarships at my college? What about the anonymous donor who took care of Tom's and my seminary tuition the month we were fretting over our finances?

Take a few minutes and look back. Who led you to the Lord? Who taught the first class you were part of in church? Who contributed to your discipleship? Who gave money to build the building where your family gathers to worship? Who wrote books that impacted your maturity as a disciple?

When I consider the indispensability of others, I also take a look around. What single great thing can I say I did by myself? I may speak—but others have spoken before me and poured thoughts into me. I may coordinate retreats and events, but what would they be without registration, decorations, setup, and cleanup? Take a few minutes to consider your most recent success. What was that success? Who contributed to the success? What might have happened had you not had them with you in that success?

And finally I take a look forward. Who will be here when I am gone? One thing Tom enjoys telling our church staff is that none of us are indispensable. If any one of us were to be taken to heaven this week, God's work would continue on. Take a few minutes to look forward. Who will be following you in ministry? What are you doing to pour into their success? Where will your children be when you are gone? When you are long gone, what echoes of your voice will these people hear in their hearts?

Humility is not weakness. Humility is strength harnessed by the love of Christ. When you embrace humility, you will win battles that wage against your church.

SERVANTHOOD IS SIGNIFICANT

Bowman wrote,

> If obedience is our motive, and humility our attitude, then serving must be our action. In ministry, we are tempted to view others

> as existing to benefit and serve us. Power, perks, and position, considered signets of success, drain the servant's soul. We are enticed to lead by the power of our position, while Jesus' yardstick is servanthood.[2]

Several years ago I went to lunch with my husband and our worship pastor. We saw a member of our church sharing a meal with his sister. A few weeks prior to this lunch our church hosted a benefit concert for this man's son (his sister's nephew). Over $100,000 was raised to help offset the costs of surgery where the little boy's legs were to be amputated. The benefit concert was a tremendous success. There were several famous country singers, lots of donations from businesses, and a huge outpouring of community support.

Deena, the sister of our church member, was praising us for our church's generosity and for Tom's leadership when Tom said, "I want you to meet Chip—"

She interrupted Tom and said, "Oh yes, I know Chip! You're the sound man!"

"He's our worship pastor," Tom finished.

Deena was taken aback. "The worship pastor! I had no idea! I was just bossing you around all over the place the other night! I'm so sorry."

Chip responded, "No! That is fine! I was the sound man."

Chip is one of the humblest worship pastors I've ever known. Because our church is near Nashville, Chip leads a choir that has included famous worship leaders, songwriters, and singers. His band is made up of instrumentalists who travel with famous country singers. And Chip doesn't think a thing about having them there. Chip simply serves God's kingdom work. And if that commitment to servanthood means punching buttons on the sound equipment, he is fine with that. On many occasions Chip invites one of the other worship leaders to lead worship while he plays drums in the background.

If you want to win the battles in your church, ask yourself this question, "How can I serve my church?"

When we first came to Thompson Station, Tom and I set up the chairs in the Sunday school rooms and cleaned the bathrooms ourselves. He mowed the grass and I washed our one and only window with paper towels and Windex. Back then we were thrilled to do those chores.

A few years ago we were hosting VBS, and somebody came hollering to me that the toilet was overflowing in the boys' bathroom. By this time we were a church running upward toward a thousand people, and the first thought in my head was, "What does that have to do with me? Surely there is someone in the house who can plunge a toilet!" But quickly I was reminded that a toilet plunger might be God's tool for me—and off I went to take care of that mess.

What can you do to serve your church? I keep a toilet plunger in my office just to remind me that if I want to win spiritual battles in my church, I must embrace the attitude of a servant. It is good to ask yourself, "Have I plunged a toilet lately?"

CONCLUSION

The Enemy will never let up on his assault against God's church. He has to keep his eyes on the church because the church is his greatest foe. Jesus told Peter that the gates of hell would not prevail against His church (Matthew 16:18).

Win the battle in your church. Be a woman who is mindful of who you are in Christ. Ask God to keep you focused on His heart so that you won't be distracted by activities and arguments that mean little to Him. Become others-centered, and as you do, realize that obedience, humility, and servanthood are significant.

Satan Targets My Church

How might you encourage your church?

Which leaders at your church need to be encouraged? How might you encourage them?

Read Matthew 16:13–20. What kind of power has been entrusted to the church?

Pray this prayer:

Father, I know that you love your church. Please increase my love for your church. Help me to understand the role I play and the ministry I fulfill. Teach me how to be an encourager and a servant to the Body of Christ where I worship.

SHARPEN YOUR SWORD

You are part of the Body of Christ. 1 Corinthians 12:12
Jesus prayed for unity in the church. John 17:20–23
Jesus commanded that we die to self. Luke 9:23–24
The Lord will fight for you. Exodus 14:14

Commit the Word to memory: Take time to review the verses you've previously memorized. Do this weekly.

PART FOUR

VICTORY IS MINE

Yes, God knew the consequences that would follow when Satan was cast out of heaven. He knew the temptation that Satan would bring to man, the crown of His creation. He foresaw the evil and conflict that would be fomented in the world. But God's love was so amazing, He went ahead with creation, knowing the battle that would ensue. He was not responsible for Satan's rebellion and self-serving motives that catapulted him from His holy presence, but God was fully aware of the continual warfare to which we would be subjected. But even before the foundation of the world, redemption was planned, and victory was assured—not just ultimately or theoretically but as a daily reality to those who are in Christ.[1]

JERRY RANKIN, *SPIRITUAL WARFARE: THE BATTLE FOR GOD'S GLORY*

Chapter Twelve

Who I Am in Christ

> Therefore if anyone is in Christ, *he is* a new creature; the old things passed away; behold, new things have come.
>
> 2 Corinthians 5:17 nasb

Many books have been written on the subject of our identity in Christ. Most of the New Testament deals with the believer's identity in Christ. But even with many books on the subject and the truths plainly stated in the Word of God, we continue to believe lies. Believing these lies gives the Enemy an edge. And when we believe the lies, we lose the battles the Enemy wages against us. The problem with most of us is that we do not take the time to grasp the reality and the freedom of our new life in Christ.

In Neil Anderson's book *The Bondage Breaker* he explains how determined Satan is to keep us captive by blinding us to the truth of our freedom in Christ:

> Before we received Christ, we were slaves to sin. Now because of Christ's work on the cross, sin's power over us has been broken.

> Satan has no right of ownership or authority over us. He is a defeated foe, but he is committed to keeping us from realizing that. The father of lies can block your effectiveness as a Christian if he can deceive you into believing that you are nothing but the product of your past—subject to sin, prone to failure, and controlled by your habits.[1]

When we embrace the truth of who we are in Christ, the devil loses his grip on us. In this chapter I am borrowing a fictional story I wrote in my book *Women Touched by Jesus*.[2] The woman caught in adultery had an intimate, raw encounter with Jesus. If we place ourselves in her sandals, we might discover the truth of who we are in Christ. And when we choose to embrace the amazing reality of this remarkable relationship, we will be empowered to become victorious warriors no matter how persistent or how revolting our Enemy proves to be.

A WOMAN CAUGHT

Read John 8:1–11 for the biblical account of the encounter this woman had with Jesus. The following, though based on this Scripture passage, is fiction.

The sun began to peek over the corner of the night. She used to love this time of day, the dawning of newness with promises of pleasure. Now she only wished for endless night—cloaked in darkness where nothing really mattered. Night for Becca consisted of putting her body into mechanical obedience as she sought to steal perhaps a tiny morsel of some sort of wicked worth. Becca was reconciled to the fact that delivering physical pleasure to powerful ople was the only thing she had to offer. It paid well, and she ved.

could still smell the foul odor of onions and fish. He'd enjoyed his dinner prior to his after-dinner exercise.

She couldn't even remember his name . . . not that it mattered anyway. Suddenly there was a noise outside her door. It sounded like men, lots of them. He cursed, pulled the covers from the pallet, and stumbled out the back. She didn't even have time to grab one of the discarded blankets he dropped in his haste as the men burst through the door and pressed in toward her. They stared as she groped for anything to cover herself. Any one of them might have sought her services in the dark of the night. But here in full daylight they huffed and scoffed in disgust. But none of them looked away.

With a pompous shout the leader of the men said, "Woman, you will come with us! God will deal with your sin today!"

She shook violently as she surveyed the room. There was no escape. The men were at the front and back doors, and they were not about to budge. She winced as two of them stepped forward and grabbed her arms in a grip that made her heart give up any hope of mercy. As two men yanked her from the pallet, a third shoved her robe to her chest, nearly knocking her off her feet. She didn't remember putting it on. They dragged her from her house, and she stubbed her toe as they shoved her across the threshold. Bruises began to form on her arms where their fingers dug into her flesh, and she looked at the ground.

I wonder what stoning feels like. I wonder if they'll knock me out first with a large rock to the head and mercifully let me lie unconscious before I die. Or will they pelt me with little rocks, bruise every inch of my body, and make sport of me? I wonder if dying hurts as bad as living this shell of a life I've lived. Becca's thoughts ran wild.

Eyes . . . she couldn't get the eyes out of her mind. Men never looked at her with warmth. Their eyes always communicated one of two things: savage hunger or arrogant disgust. Last night, and so many nights before, she had seen in his eyes savage hunger. Today and so many days before it was arrogant disgust. As the pictures of hundreds of faces, those of both men and women, flashed before her mind's eyes, Becca was suddenly shoved to the ground. She dared not look up, but she felt the eyes of many looking down at her.

"Teacher, this woman was caught in the act of adultery. The law of Moses commanded us to stone such women. Now what do you say?" One of the religious rule keepers haughtily shouted out her sin. But Becca didn't hear the anger in his voice; she was immediately distracted by the one he called "Teacher."

Teacher—did they say "Teacher"? she asked herself. Becca had heard of this teacher. Her cousin came to visit her a few months ago and had told her about this *teacher*. "You need to come meet this man they call Jesus!" she said.

"Oh, come on. He can't be so different than all the other men!" Becca had answered back.

"No, Becca, this man is different! Just wait until you see His eyes," her cousin exclaimed.

"I've seen men's eyes. They hold hunger that is easily satisfied with flesh, or they hold disgust that is only satisfied with shame. I've no need for the eyes of men," Becca responded.

"Becca, all I know is that this man is different. His eyes are full of compassion, and I've only seen Him heal with His hands. Please come with me to where He's teaching today," her cousin pleaded.

"Not today." Becca didn't feel like going. Her hope had died many years before. If there was a God, and if He was as the Pharisees described Him to be, she had long ago out-sinned His mercy. But here she was, tossed to the ground like a discarded bedroll, huddled in a ball at the feet of Jesus. Becca couldn't resist the urge to peek at this man. Timidly she lifted her eyes and glanced over to the one they called "Teacher."

He wasn't so big, and His clothes were not fancy. He was very [illegible]ke the men who'd paraded into her house this morning. The [illegible]r was surrounded by common people; men, women, and even [illegible] were sitting right up close to Him. He sat with authority [illegible] to be in the middle of a deep discussion when He was interrupted by her captors. Becca couldn't see His face, only His body as He bent down and started drawing in the sand.

What is He doing? she wondered.

"What do you say? The very act—we caught her in the very act! She was still in her sin-filled bed when we found her!" Her accusers went on and on.

But Jesus didn't say *anything*, He simply continued to draw in the sand.

Becca wondered, *Is He ignoring them? What is He doing?* She had to admire the way He refused to be upset by their interruption. Finally, He stopped drawing. He straightened up and said to them, "If any one of you is without sin, let him be the first to throw a stone at her." Then He stooped down again and continued writing in the sand.

Becca wondered at His answer and almost chuckled to herself at His calm response to what was obviously a trick question. Now she knew why these arrogant religious hypocrites hated Him so. In just the few minutes she'd been in His presence, she sensed the power of His authority that would not be coerced into playing their religious games. But because she understood the arrogance of the Pharisees, she still fully expected the stoning to begin any second . . . so she merely smiled at His clever answer and braced herself for the impact of the first stone.

After a few seconds of silence she noticed the oldest of the Pharisees sigh deeply and shuffle off away from the others. His departure began a quiet exit of all her accusers, one by one. She watched in amazement as they silently walked away. Before long she was the only one still there. She'd had her head lowered in shame. Oh, how she wished for something in which to hide her face. Unfortunately, in their haste, the religious leaders had only grabbed her robe to cover her nakedness and hadn't even thought to provide a covering for her hair. Suddenly she felt all alone and dirty. It was as if she were naked and exposed before a King.

Out of curiosity Becca lifted her head, expecting Him to look at her with eyes full of righteous indignation and judgment. But as she timidly lifted her face to look at Him, He put His hand on her chin and raised her head until she could look Him directly in His eyes. The minute she made eye contact with Him, she heard Him say, "Woman, where are they? Has no one condemned you?"

Time stood still. Becca lost herself in the perfect love of Jesus. Her cousin's description of Him came flooding back to her. She'd never seen such compassion and total acceptance before. As she gazed into the window of His soul, all her sin, all her shame—her past hurts, her wrong choices, her guilt—all of it was there. Becca swallowed the fear that had crept up in her throat and realized that she was standing before a purely holy, righteous man. And although she knew her sin was ever before her, somehow His eyes reflected nothing other than complete, unreserved, total acceptance and love.

Becca somehow squeaked her answer past the turmoil in her heart, "No one, sir."

She couldn't take her eyes from His. Before His next words ever formed in His mouth, she knew that whatever He said, He meant. And as she marveled in His glory, she heard Him say, "Then neither do I condemn you. Go now and sin no more."

More precious words had never been spoken.

WHO I AM IN CHRIST

I'm not sure what circumstances led "Becca" to Jesus that day. I've no idea if she was a prostitute, a desperate housewife, or even the wife of one of the Pharisees who'd been caught in a sordid affair. t I don't really have to know her story in order to hear what had echoing in her mind:

cca, you are worthless! You don't have any talent! You Your best effort will never be good enough and you will othing!"

Have you any lies like that bouncing around in between your ears? I do! When I was a young teen, I ambitioned to be the first woman president of the United States. In the tenth grade I started my political career; I ran for sophomore class secretary. I might have won, but I misspelled *secretary* on all my campaign posters and didn't even notice the mistake until our English teacher made an example out of it in front of the class.

"Your best effort is not good enough and you will amount to nothing!" I heard the raspy whisper in my ears. Needless to say, my brief political career ended in an embarrassing defeat. I don't know why I struggle with these voices of defeat that clamor in my head. Listening to them has cost me dearly, and if I'm not careful they will drive me to look to others to receive endorsement of my self-worth. God knew these lies were threatening to incapacitate me—and He had greater plans for me than to live my days on earth held captive by their venom. He's got better plans for you too.

Jeremiah 29:11 is my life verse: " 'For I know the plans I have for you,' declares the Lord. 'Plans to *prosper* you and *not to harm you*—plans to *give you a hope and a future.*' "

These are the plans God has for each one of us. You are reading this right now because God wants to remind you of His plans. God wants to rid you of the negative thoughts you battle in your mind.

MY LIFE SENTENCE

I asked Jesus into my heart when I was eleven, and He immediately went to work to eliminate my toxic way of thinking. My first year at youth camp, the summer after seventh grade, we studied a book by Grady Nutt titled *Being Me: Self, You Bug Me!*

I don't remember anything about the Bible studies, worship services, or small group discussions. I don't even remember what we did for fun, but I do remember this sentence from that book. Where Jeremiah 29:11 is my life verse, this has become my life sentence: "I am a person of worth created in the image of God to relate and live."[3]

I AM A PERSON OF WORTH

You are God's idea. In Psalm 139:14 David praised God for this truth: "I will praise You, because I have been remarkably and wonderfully made. Your works are wonderful, and I know [this] very well" (HCSB).

You are remarkably and wonderfully made! God knit you together in your mother's womb. Before she even knew she carried you in her body, God was weaving you together. You were His secret. When no one knew of you, God was meticulously working out every fearful and wonderful part of *you*! Can you agree with David's thoughts when he pondered this truth? Would you be willing to shout, "I am remarkably and wonderfully made! All your works, Lord, are wonderful! I know this very well!"?

I'm not talking about what you've done to your body by exercising your own free will. I'm talking about the miraculous, intricate, amazing body God gave you. It is His gift and He considers it "very good." I am convinced if we, the daughters of the King of Glory, would look at our reflections in the mirrors each morning and shout with David, "Your works are wonderful and I know [this] very well!" we would become stronger warriors on the battlefield of our lives.

What about it? Why don't you try it the next time you gaze at yourself in the mirror? "Lord, I am remarkably and wonderfully made! All your works are wonderful! I know this very well!" Then thank God for life . . . your life . . . the one He chose for you. I dare
ı. And the next time someone compliments you, don't respond
"This old thing?" Instead smile, clap your hands together, and
'I am fearfully and wonderfully made! I thought this dress
iod's great work too! That's why I bought it!" Just see
ponse might do!

As I grew physically, I gradually came to grips with God's opinion of me. The night I asked Jesus into my heart, the deciding factor was the value God placed on my soul. He spoke in His gentle yet powerful voice and allowed me to understand that if I had been the only one in the entire world who chose to sin, God would have sent Jesus to die for me. That meant I was valuable to Him. Then as I grew in my relationship with God, I came to understand the next part of my life sentence.

CREATED IN THE IMAGE OF GOD

I am a person of worth *created in the image of God*. . . .

Image is an interesting phenomenon in our culture. As women we wrestle with the images of beauty and success. The source of our wrestling comes in the discrepancy between what the world calls beautiful and successful and what God's Word declares to be beautiful and successful.

God is not looking for the world's beauty nor does He measure our worth by the world's standard for success. When God looks at our lives, He is looking for mirror images of His Son. We were created in the very image of God (remember from chapter 1 that our lives are God-breathed). Then, we were redeemed by the sacrificial death of His Son. Today, when God looks at us, He wants to see himself in our eyes. What does that mean? How can we reflect the image of Christ?

> Therefore be imitators of God, as beloved children; and walk in love, just as Christ also loved you and gave Himself up for us, an offering and a sacrifice to God as a fragrant aroma.
>
> EPHESIANS 5:1–2 NASB

Paul told the Ephesians that they ought to become imitators of God so that they would reflect the truth that they were indeed dearly loved children. One of the joys of parenthood is watching your children grow. Several times Tom and I have commented abo how amazing it is to see both of us reflected in our three children. Of course Mikel, Kaleigh, and TJ have their own unique qualities that are original with them, but many of our good (and bad) traits are evident in them physically, socially, emotionally, and even spiritually. Even when they try not to, our three children reflect the image of Tom and me in their lives.

They are a whole lot like us because they're made of our DNA. They are also like us because they spent the formative years of their lives in our care. And they are like us because there are times when they actually see characteristics in us that they admire, and they choose to mimic those things.

God's already done the miraculous work of making us His sons and daughters. When we asked Jesus into our hearts, God placed the Holy Spirit there. Paul tells us in 2 Corinthians 1:22 that God gave us His Spirit as a deposit—a guarantee of our eternal life to come. We were "born again."

God allowed us to be born of the Spirit. He placed His spiritual DNA in our hearts.

If you have received Jesus, you are undeniably a child of God—a dearly beloved child according to Ephesians 5:1. Now you must do your part. As you spend time with your heavenly Father studying His Word and praying, you will become more like Him. Then, as you choose to admire Him and allow His characteristics to intentionally be put into practice in your behavior, you will become a beautiful reflection of Christ.

Do you buy into lies that attack the image God's given you? There's no room for poor self-esteem in God's kingdom work. When suffer from poor self-esteem, we forget who we are in Christ, ve focus too much on ourselves. As long as we are preoccupied rselves, we are looking in the wrong mirrors. Our attention wrong "god." God longs for us to take our eyes off the ourselves . . . and off other people. He's urging us to esus. Do you remember the simple chorus?

> Turn your eyes upon Jesus,
> Look full in His wonderful face.
> And the things of earth will grow strangely dim,
> In the light of His glory and grace.[4]

The truth of my life sentence doesn't stop there.

TO RELATE

I am a person of worth created in the image of God *to relate*. . . .

God did not create us to live life alone. We've already discussed this truth in the chapters that dealt with significant relationships in our lives. You cannot fully understand who you are in Christ apart from who you are in relationship to others. In fact, if you were to ask me who I am, I would say that I'm Tom McCoy's wife; TJ, Mikel, and Kaleigh's mother; Sharon, Mitzi, and Amy's sister; and Mike and Lounette's daughter. I might add that I am the prayer and women's minister at Thompson Station Church, a conference leader, and the author of several books. ALL of these descriptions of me are dependent upon others.

In Grady Nutt's book *Being Me*, he borrows from another book you've most likely heard of, *I'm OK, You're OK*. He states,

> I'm OK, you're OK. This is the position of hope which best exemplifies wisdom, self-appreciation and maturity. It is a position based on thought, faith, commitment and decision. I'm OK, you're OK acknowledges both the worth in self and the worth in neighbor. It further enables a person to trust what he knows of himself to what he knows of another.[5]

This is the lesson Jesus was teaching the religious leaders when He said, "If any one of you is without sin, let him be the first to throw a stone at her!"

You see, when the teachers of the law brought the adulterous woman to Jesus and demanded that they "stone such a one," they shouted, "I'm okay! She is not, and what are *you* going to do about it?"

To which the woman most likely responded in her own mind, "They're okay, I am not, and I wonder what stoning feels like."

Satan holds God's people hostage with thoughts of inferiority all the time—especially women! How many women do you know who do not serve in the church, or pursue their dreams, or offer to help because they do not feel worthy? When Satan holds you captive by feelings of insecurity and inferiority, he robs God's

A Note From the Trenches

I finally had to change the tone of my quiet time the other day. For the first month of my daughter's departure, I wrote to her. I penned letters that she may never read; then I opened the Bible and talked to God. This daily practice helped me process my thoughts and feelings. Finally the morning came when I had nothing left to say to her. So I shut her book and opened the Bible. For a few days my quiet times were filled with whys, what ifs, and "You've got to do something about that boy!" But then God told me I had whined long enough. He encouraged me to return to a discipline I embrace often in my quiet time. It is the discipline of praying for an hour. I pray for a solid hour by breaking my hour into five-minute segments. The first five minutes are dedicated to praising God.

This week I opened my Bible and the thought came to me to look up verses that reminded me of how much God loved me. During my praise time (which went much longer than five minutes) I bathed myself in the love of God. Some of the verses I meditated on that morning are these: Isaiah 54:10; John 15:9, 13; 1 John 4:14–15.

kingdom of your gifts and your influence. He robs God's kingdom of the incredible contributions you might make while here on earth. And those contributions you would make would reveal His glory among the nations.

God's Word sets you free. His Word has the power to break the chains the Enemy uses to hold God's children captive. Consider these truths from God's Word. Read them aloud.

Psalm 139:14: "I am fearfully and wonderfully made!"

Ephesians 1:4: "I am chosen by God!"

First John 3:1: "I am loved by God."

If you had the privilege of growing up in the church, you know the song "Jesus loves me, this I know . . . for the Bible tells me so!"[6] Sing that song right now.

The best way I can love you is to first embrace the love my heavenly Father has for me. I am loved. Say that aloud with me: "I am loved."

TO LIVE

I am a person of worth, created in the image of God to relate *and to live*.

Who am I in Christ? I am a person of worth created in the image of God—to relate and to live. To really live! To live the life God created me to live. I am a person of worth, created in the image of God to relate and *to live*. How are we to do that?

The woman who was caught in the very act of adultery learned something significant about life the day she was brought before Jesus by the Pharisees. Even though she was an adulteress . . . even though many of her dreams had shattered into a zillion pieces . . . even though her reputation was tarnished . . . even though society regarded her as an outcast . . . even though other women looked down on her . . . even though she might not have had friends . . . and even though her sin was displayed in the temple courts . . .

she still had a choice. God gave "the woman caught in adultery" a choice. With Jesus' amazing grace, this woman was offered a precious gift—the gift of ***life.***

> "Woman, has no one condemned you?" Jesus asked.
>
> "No, sir, not one," the woman responded.
>
> "Then neither do I condemn you," Jesus said.
>
> SEE JOHN 8:10–11

Let those words sink into your heart. Have you a secret sin you try desperately to hide? Are you caught in addiction? Been wounded by divorce? Scarred by abuse? Do you harbor unforgiveness, bitterness, or shame? Are the voices in your head clamoring loudly to be heard? Do the people surrounding you tell you to adapt to your life of broken dreams?

Jesus says to you, my friend, "God did not send me into your world to condemn you, but to save you! If you will believe in me, you are not condemned" (see John 3:16–17).

Jesus loves you. He does not condemn you today. Instead, He stretches out His nail-scarred hands and longs to wrap them around your battle-scarred heart. He wants to take your heart of stone and replace it with a heart of flesh. Jesus wants to offer you an exchange: your old, dead, defeated, and disappointed life for a new, vibrant life secure in Christ.

All you have to do is believe and receive. Believe that Jesus is the Son of God. Receive the gift of His sacrificial death—His paying the penalty for your sin on that cruel Roman cross. Ask for His perfect forgiveness and place your yesterday, your today, and your tomorrow in His capable hands.

Perhaps you invited Jesus to be your Savior many years ago. But somewhere along the way you made one wrong turn that led to another, then another and . . . Aren't you ready to come home? Believe God when He says to you again today, "If you will believe in me, you are not condemned." Ask Him for His perfect forgiveness and embrace a future that is not tainted by your past. The door to His heart is still wide open for you. He didn't change the locks while you were gone; He didn't hide the key. Come on home; He's eager to see you again.

You are not condemned; you have a life to live! Start living it today!

I am a person of worth (valued by God so much that He sent the crown prince of heaven to pay my redemption price) created in the image of God (His very own daughter) to relate (with you, with them, with women like this one huddled at Jesus' feet, with the people in India who believe in reincarnation) and to live! (A life that is full, complete, lacking in no good thing—as I demonstrate the love of God every step of the way.)

I am loved. That truth alone will send your Enemy on the run.

Who I Am in Christ

Do you have some lies running rampant in your head?

What does God's Word say about you?

Read Ephesians 1:3–11 and 2:1–10. Think about what you've read.

Pray this prayer:

Oh, God, let the reality that you tenderly created me in your very own image penetrate my mind and my heart. Father, forgive me for being so preoccupied with myself that I've failed to be about your business. Release me from fear and insecurity. I will rise from the dirt, brush off my skirt, go forth and sin no more. I know that I am already a mighty warrior not because of what I bring to the battlefield but rather because of who I am in you.

SHARPEN YOUR SWORD

You are a new creation. 2 Corinthians 5:17
God has a plan for your life. Jeremiah 29:11
You are fearfully and wonderfully made! Psalm 139
You are chosen by God! Ephesians 1:4
You are loved by God. 1 John 3:1

Commit the Word to memory: If you struggle with issues of self-esteem, choose one of these verses and write it in permanent ink on the palm of your hand. (That's a bit more discreet than writing it on your forehead.) Repeat the verse daily. You will have it memorized by the time the ink fades away.

Chapter Thirteen

How I Defeat My Enemy

> For the word of God is living and active. Sharper than any double-edged sword, it penetrates even to dividing soul and spirit, joints and marrow; it judges the thoughts and attitudes of the heart.
>
> Hebrews 4:12

There is a tool that the Enemy uses against you—one that is powerful because it is personal; that is, your very own flesh. In order to experience consistent victory in the battles that wage against you, you must recognize the victory God gave you to subdue the flesh. In this chapter, you will learn how the Enemy entices your flesh and how the Spirit gives you the power to overcome temptation.

There is also a weapon God has given you that is powerful because it too is personal; that is, His very own Word. The writer of Hebrews told us that God's Word is active, sharper than any double-edged sword, and that it is able to penetrate deep as it judges the thoughts and attitudes of the heart (see Hebrews 4:12). In this chapter, you will learn how to wield this powerful weapon in your battles against the Enemy.

THE POWER OF THE FLESH

"Spiritual warfare is not so much about demon possession, territorial spirits, or generational bondage as it is overcoming Satan's lies and deceits in your own life."[1]

I completely agree with Jerry Rankin, who made that statement in his book *Spiritual Warfare: The Battle for God's Glory*. Satan is a liar! In chapter 5, we discussed the fact that Jesus called him the Father of Lies (John 8:44).

Satan is a subtle—not blatant—liar. His motivation is deception. He longs to deceive you with half-truths and shortcuts. Ron Hutchcraft said this about Satan and his lies:

> The devil's basic strategy is really pretty simple: get you obsessed with the prize you might get so you're blind to the trap you're walking into. He'll convince you that it's "just this once," "just a little," "it won't hurt." Lies. All lies. Jesus exposed the devil when He said, he is the "father of lies" and "there is no truth in him" (John 8:44). He is, as Jesus said, the "thief" who comes only to "steal, kill and destroy." You will not ultimately get what he seems to be offering—the satisfaction, the life, the excitement, the relief. It's just Satan's bait to take you captive and ruin everything he can in your life. But he'll promise you anything to get you to walk into his trap.[2]

SATAN STILL LIES TODAY

I want you to repeat after me: "Satan is a liar." How has he lied to you? Don't miss the fact that Eve lived in a perfect world. And even in that perfect world she lost the battle with temptation. I think it's important to realize what you're battling against.

We battle with temptation—not with sin. And temptation is a struggle between our will (what I like to call our "God-directed want-to") and our earthly desires, which are our appetites, feelings, passions—those things in which we find satisfaction in the here and now. Our earthly desires include the stuff that stimulates. Things like coffee, chocolate, cupcakes, entertainment, love stories, warm embraces, kisses in the moonlight . . . you get my drift. These things are not bad in and of themselves—but when you have thoughts about the married man with whom you work—Satan is at work. When you'd rather read your romance novel than work on romance in your marriage—Satan is at work. When entertainment takes the place of time with God—Satan is at work. You get the idea.

When these earthly desires play tug-of-war with your spiritual will, Paul calls them the "lust of the flesh" (Galatians 5:16 KJV). When Adam and Eve occupied Eden, the only thing Satan could use to appeal to their earthly desire was one fruit tree among many. We ought to be humbled by this story when we realize that perfect Eve was snookered by Satan for a bite of fruit. How many of us need to eat more fruit daily? And how much more vulnerable are we when Satan has worldly lures like mass media, the Internet, gourmet markets and restaurants, alcohol, prescription drugs, nicotine, caffeine, daytime television, pornography, texting, and Facebook at his disposal? I don't know about you—but I just *wish* I only wanted a bite of fruit!

A LESSON IN TEMPTATION

Satan has both the world around us and the flesh within us to use against us in this spiritual battle. Let's go one last time to the very beginning and see why Eve succumbed to temptation. Read Genesis 3:6: "When the woman saw that the fruit was good for food and pleasing to the eye, and also desirable for gaining wisdom, she took some and ate it."

First, Eve saw that the fruit was "good for food." Was the fruit good? NO! This fruit was terrible! But it must have been tasty. How often do we yield to the things that tempt our physical appetites? I've read, listened to, and even participated in several weight-loss programs: First Place, Weight Watchers, Weigh Down, Prism, Nutrisystem, etc. In lots of these diets they tell me that when I eat more than my body needs I am feeding myself emotionally. While that might be true, the reason I am eating the "maestro chocolate bars" my sister mailed me last week is simply because they *taste good*!

Your Enemy will always tempt you with something that delivers *something*. If it didn't satisfy (temporarily) some appetite in you, then it wouldn't be tempting! But what Satan offers never delivers completely. His morsels always rely on shortcuts and/or immediate gratification. And although they do satisfy a bit, they leave your deeper needs (for love, peace, acceptance, etc.) not only unmet but stirred up and agitated, demanding all the more. Satan's lure has only one goal: to take you captive and eventually ruin your life.

Remember Jesus' temptation? The devil promised Jesus that if He would bow down *that very minute* He could rule the earth without suffering the cross. Satan promised Jesus a shortcut that would *not* accomplish what Jesus came to do. Consider addictions. What do they deliver? Immediate relief, a "buzz," the dulling of the senses, excitement. With what to follow? Remorse, regret, loss, despair, depression, and eventually death.

Eve's fruit might have been good for food—but it was definitely bad for the soul.

Second, Eve's fruit was "pleasing to the eye." Her fruit appealed to her. It was pretty! It looked innocent enough—even enticing. Here is where the world has allowed Satan to cloak himself dangerously. Caricatures would have you believe that he is a dragon surrounded by fire, or a red monster with horns and a forked tail, or even a slimy snake ready to strike. But most often the devil comes in the form of a compassionate man who is eager to hear how your man isn't measuring up . . . or a chocolate cupcake piled high with icing that promises to make you feel better for yelling at your kids this morning . . . or a friend eager to hear the intimate details of your problems at home so that she can offer her compassion and remind you that you are too good to put up with that. Never does the object of temptation reveal itself to be as wicked as it truly is.

Third, Eve saw that the fruit was "desirable for gaining wisdom." This fruit appealed to Eve because it was going to give her something God chose not to give her. Eating this fruit would open for Eve a world that was off limits according to God. Satan tempted Eve with the ploy of portraying God as a killjoy. How does this happen today?

I know one woman who told me, "I read that book that told me how to pray for my husband and I prayed all those prayers, but God never answered me. When Keith came along he gave me what my husband did not. God let me down—so I chose the affair. So what?! I have found 'real love' now—and that's something God never let me have."

I know another who started working out for her health—but she got addicted to the exercise and now eats, sleeps, and drinks to "good health." She's had her body lifted, tucked, fluffed, and toned. She's no longer interested in bringing her children to church, giving to missions, reading God's Word, or developing relationships with other believers. Her body became her god.

And I know another who reads romance novels at the rate of one a day. She has few friends, little interaction with others outside her workplace, no meaningful activities that she is engaged in, and she has lost all hope of ever sharing life with a man.

The forbidden fruits that appeal to our earthly desires trick us into thinking they can offer us something God has chosen to refuse. When we live to satisfy our flesh—that part of us that shouts to be fed, recognized, properly appreciated, satisfied, and adored—we become lovers of self. And when our self-love chokes out reverence, worship, love, and honor for God, we allow our own self-centered lives to rob God of His glory.

THE FLESH

Temptation targets the flesh. *Sarx* is the Greek word for flesh. It is the deadly enemy of the *pneuma*, which is the Greek word for Spirit—that part of man that fellowships with God. We are born of the Spirit when we accept Christ as Savior (see John 3).

1. **To live in the flesh is the precise opposite to being a Christian.**
2. **To be in the flesh is to be under sin.**
3. **The flesh is the great enemy of the abundant life.**
4. **The flesh must be eliminated and eradicated. Why? Because the flesh serves the law of sin (Romans 7:25); the flesh blinds us to truth (1 Corinthians 3:1–3); the flesh cannot please God (Romans 8:8); and the flesh is hostile to God (Romans 8:9).**[3]

The flesh is what we have allowed ourselves to become in contrast with what God meant us to be. The flesh is human nature as it has become through sin. The flesh is what Adam and Eve hid in the bushes.

Consider this quote:

> Temptation would be powerless to affect man, unless there was something already in man to respond to temptation. Sin could gain no foothold in a man's mind and heart and soul and life unless there was an enemy within the gates who was willing to open the door to sin. The flesh is exactly the bridgehead through which sin invades the human personality.[4]

Flesh and Our Physical Bodies

The flesh is not synonymous with our physical bodies. Before they sinned, Adam and Eve paraded around the garden in their birthday suits unashamed. It was only after they experienced the shame of their sin that they felt the need to cover up. Their physical bodies were just as clean, beautiful, and "right" before God as they had been before. But their minds (thinking) and hearts (feeling) were stained by sin. The flesh is that part of us that behaves independently of God from within our thoughts (minds) and attitudes (hearts). While our physical bodies are natural, earthly, and destined to decay, they are neither good nor bad. They are merely the "earth suits" that transport us about while we're living here.

In Jennifer Kennedy Dean's Bible study *The Life-Changing Power in the Blood of Christ*, she teaches a powerful truth regarding the flesh. Her truth is the basis of the following discussion of the flesh.[5]

Your flesh is any point at which you're not allowing the Spirit life to flow through you. Your flesh is in operation when you are in command rather than the Spirit of Christ in you. God is determined to "flush the flesh" out of you. He does this by allowing you crucifixion moments.

CRUCIFIXION MOMENT

Because of His great love for you, the Father is building experiences into your life that will cause your flesh to come to the surface and be exposed. When you find yourself in a situation in which your flesh is exposed, you have come to a "crucifixion moment." At this moment, you choose to act according to your flesh pattern (and cut off the flow of resurrection life), or to crucify the flesh (and allow Christ's resurrection life to flow through you).

In other words, just say "No!" to the flesh and the resurrection life will *flow*!

The people who win spiritual battles today are those who have mastered the art of denying the flesh so that they might live by God's power. Victorious warriors have learned to crucify the flesh.

Have you ever wondered why God allows temptation to come into our lives? Satan tempts us to defeat us, but God allows him to tempt us to grow us. God's method of training is to allow temptation to come your way; His intent is that the temptation will bring you to maturity.

> Consider it all joy, my brethren, when you encounter various trials, knowing that the testing of your faith produces endurance. And let endurance have its perfect result, so that you may be perfect and complete, lacking in nothing.
>
> JAMES 1:2–4 NASB

Does God want to "trip you up"? No, never! "God is faithful; he will not let you be tempted beyond what you can bear" (1 Corinthians 10:13).

WHY SOME PEOPLE CRUMBLE UNDER PRESSURE

Temptation is not sin. Temptation does not necessarily lead to sin. However, no sin comes into being without temptation. So what is the process by which temptation becomes sin? "Each one is tempted when, by his own evil desire, he is dragged away and enticed. Then, after desire has conceived, it gives birth to sin" (James 1:14–15).

Strong, intense desire is built into us by our Creator. God created us with a deep need for love and acceptance so that we would have an appetite for Him. However, our God-created desires become misdirected when we seek to have them met outside of God. Anything outside of God only meets the surface of the need, provides only temporary relief, and must be repeated over and over again.

> As when a hungry man dreams he is eating, but he awakens, and his hunger remains; as when a thirsty man dreams that he is drinking, but he awakens faint, with his thirst unquenched.
>
> Isaiah 29:8

The very need or desire that should have turned us to God has turned us away from Him. Instead of being freed from our need by having it eternally met, we become enslaved to our need by having it forever unsatisfied. We have then a misdirected desire. It has taken root in us. It becomes a root of unrighteousness, and it grows a fruit called sin. "By his own evil desire, he is dragged away and enticed" (James 1:14).

This misdirected desire has developed a magnetic attraction to something in the world. We'll call this object or situation in the world a stimulus. Satan has dangled bait in front of you. Bait such as Eve's fruit, Amanda's Keith, Carol's gym, Sheila's romance novels. Your misdirected desire has taken the bait and been lured into a trap. You are dragged away by your own misdirected desire. The misdirected desire lodges itself in your "want-to." But its root is in your God-given desire to relate intimately with Him. The root becomes a root of unrighteousness (rather than righteousness) when you choose to satisfy that desire with the stimulus in the world. "After desire has conceived, it gives birth to sin" (James 1:15).

This mating results in conception, and sin is born. Sin is born of the mating between your misdirected desire and a stimulus in the world.

SO WHAT ARE WE TO DO?

Destroy the root! Once the root is gone, the stimulus in the world has nothing to mate with. Temptation forces choice. Every time we face temptation, we choose where to take our need. Will we allow God to fulfill our needs and satisfy our eternal cravings by taking Him at His Word, choosing obedience to Him and following hard after Him? Or will we take the drive-through, fast-food approach and depend on the world? Every temptation forces us deeper into the heart of the Father or anchors us more securely in the world.

In the same way that our flesh impulses become flesh patterns by repeating an action over and over again, so temptation can cause us to become fixed in the way of the Spirit by persistent choice. We can choose God over and over until He becomes our "holy habit" and the ways of the Spirit become our spontaneous choice.

We teach five holy habits in a maturity class at our church. The holy habits are:

1. **Spend time with God in His Word**
2. **Pray**
3. **Tithe**
4. **Fellowship with others**
5. **Witness**

Developing these holy habits will strengthen you for the task of choosing wisely when temptation presents the opportunity. And, because you are a child of God, you have a choice.

Satan will try to convince you that you are not strong enough to follow God once you become aware of the trap you are in. But God's Word declares you dead to sin and alive to God.

> Each of us is raised into a light-filled world by our Father so that we can see where we're going in our new grace-sovereign country. Could it be any clearer? Our old way of life was nailed to the cross with Christ, a decisive end to that sin-miserable life—no longer at sin's every beck and call! What we believe is this: If we get included in Christ's sin-conquering death, we also get included in his life-saving resurrection. We know that

> when Jesus was raised from the dead it was a signal of the end of death-as-the-end. Never again will death have the last word. When Jesus died, he took sin down with him, but alive he brings God down to us. From now on, think of it this way: *Sin speaks a dead language that means nothing to you; God speaks your mother tongue, and you hang on every word. You are dead to sin and alive to God. That's what Jesus did.*
>
> Romans 6:5–11 The Message

The Enemy has a weapon that is powerful and personal. It is your very own flesh. But God has given you the power to overcome. God's Word is true, and Satan is a liar. Choose to stand firm on the Word of God and you will win every battle every time.

THE POWER OF GOD'S WORD

Between Christmas and New Year's Day, I reflect on the past year and set goals for the next one. I do this prayerfully, and God always gives me a few goals and a word for my new year. This year one of my goals was to read biographies of some of the great missionaries. I've completed a rather large biography of Hudson Taylor's life (Taylor was a missionary to China in the 1800s) and am right now reading the biography of Amy Carmichael (missionary to India). Hudson Taylor said,

> There are three truths, 1st, That there is a God; 2nd, That He has spoken to us in the Bible; 3rd, That He means what He says. Oh the joy of trusting Him! . . . The missionary who realises these truths . . . knows that he has solid rock under his feet whatever may be his circumstances.[6]

That quote resonates in my heart because it came out of the heart of a man who lost two wives and several of his children; and he suffered tremendous physical pain throughout his life because of his response to God's call. I was disturbed by the losses suffered by the missionaries who pioneered in China. But I was more bewildered by the deep peace and overwhelming joy that seemed to develop in direct correlation to the measure of their suffering.

My Bible verse for this year was from Isaiah. God actually gave me two passages of Scripture with a promise. Remember these verses were given to me on January 1—at that time Mikel was in the middle of her senior year in high school. She had just decided to attend Union University (a great Christian college in Jackson, Tennessee), Kaleigh was in the middle of her junior year, and TJ in his freshman year in high school. I thought I was healthy, our church was growing, and we were enjoying the holiday season. Here are the Scriptures God gave me at that time:

> Forget the former things; do not dwell on the past. See, I am doing a new thing! Now it springs up; do you not perceive it? I am making a way in the desert and streams in the wasteland.
>
> Isaiah 43:18–19

> But now listen, O Jacob, my servant, Israel, whom I have chosen. This is what the Lord says—he who made you, who formed you in the womb, and who will help you: Do not be afraid, O Jacob, my servant, Jeshurun, whom I have chosen. For I will pour water on the thirsty land, and streams on the dry ground; I will pour out my Spirit on your offspring, and my blessing on your descendants. They will spring up like grass in a meadow, like poplar trees by flowing streams. One will say, "I belong to the Lord"; another will call himself by the name of Jacob; still another will write on his hand, "The Lord's," and will take the name Israel.
>
> Isaiah 44:1–5

The promise I heard from God was that the new year would be full of blessings (streams in the wasteland) and that I was going to enjoy the parenting success of "three for three." If you look closely at Isaiah 44:5, the prophet clearly referenced three different children who will embrace God in their lives. Tom and I have always prayed that when our children grow up they will each follow the Lord and live in the center of His plans for their lives. We've often said that nothing in our ministries matters more than that we pass our faith on to our children. The Word of God is powerful and personal. Only God knew, in January, how much I would need the promise of Isaiah 44:5 this year. He speaks to us through His Word. He also strengthens us with His Word when we find ourselves in the midst of battle.

On March 1 I was surprised by my cancer, but I didn't really take it personally. I was a bit miffed that I'd worked so hard to exercise and eat right (having given up Twinkies and MoonPies my entire adult life), but I humbly understood that if Lance Armstrong had cancer I was certainly not exempt. However, I rushed straight to God's Word and enjoyed many powerfully personal verses that encouraged me during that time. When the flood came to our church on May 1, we were frustrated but not despairing. The entire ordeal was more of a distraction than a discouragement. Our community came together to help us, and we discovered the word *flood* used in many passages of Scripture!

But when my daughter left home, I was knocked off my solid rock. I felt as if every promise God had ever made was destroyed by the choices of an eighteen-year-old girl. But as the dust has settled, Tom and I have "opened our mouths wide" and been fed to overflowing with God's Word. Not a day goes by that God doesn't speak specifically to me in His Word, adding promise on top of promise to what He is going to do.

Because I am in the thick of the battle, I have employed Post-it Note warfare. I print every promise God gives me (that pertains to this moment in my life) on a sticky note and then post these notes on my mirrors, walls, refrigerator, oven, microwave, pantry doors—all over my house. As we walk through the house, we speak the powerful promises of God aloud. In this practical way I take my random rampaging thoughts captive to the lordship of Christ. I make the choice minute by minute to demand that my thoughts bow down to God's Word.

Here's how this works. The Enemy would have me believe that although I came through the cancer and then the flood praising God and giving glory to His name, this time I'm going to fall flat on my face. But God's Word tells me that

> "no weapon that is formed against you will prosper; and every tongue that accuses you in judgment you will condemn. This is the heritage of the servants of the Lord, and their vindication is from Me," declares the Lord.
>
> ISAIAH 54:17 NASB

That verse is posted on the mirror in my bathroom. Now, please understand that the strength of this warfare does not come in your hearing of the Word, nor does it come in the fact that God's Word is written, that you have posted it on your walls, or that you are saying it out loud. Your strength and victory come when *you* choose to anchor your hope, your confidence, and your mind in God's Word. Take God at His Word and you will not be disappointed.

> [My word] will not return to me empty, but will accomplish what I desire and achieve the purpose for which I sent it. You will go out in joy and be led forth in peace.
>
> ISAIAH 55:11–12

I promise you that God's Word has something powerful and personal to say to you no matter what the Enemy brings your way. I have taken God at His Word for many years and have yet to find any discrepancy between how He responds to my prayers and what He says in His Word. I'm eager to see how He fulfills the promises I have posted on the walls of my home today. Just this morning He said to me, "If you remain in me and my words remain in you, ask whatever you wish, and it will be given you" (John 15:7).

That sounds to me like God is asking me to just try to see if I can find something that He cannot do! Don't forget that all God's promises are YES! "For as many as are the promises of God, in Him they are yes" (2 Corinthians 1:20 NASB).

And don't miss the next part of that verse. When we choose to believe the promises of God and respond to them with a hearty AMEN (so be it!), *then* the glory of God flows through us: "Therefore also through Him is our Amen to the glory of God through us."

And when the glory of God flows through us, the battle is won!

How I Defeat My Enemy

What does the world have to offer that you find especially appealing?

Read Philippians 4:19. What does God's Word say about God's ability to satisfy your every need? How can you *know* that you have victory over the flesh?

Pray this prayer:

Father, I often feel like Paul when he said, "I do what I don't want to do and I don't do what I want to do" (see Romans 7:14–20). However, I agree with your Word when you have said to me that I am an overcomer. I am dead to sin and alive in Christ. Please remind me of your power alive in me when I face temptation today. Show me also the Word you have for me to claim (in whatever battle you are facing today).

SHARPEN YOUR SWORD

God's Word is active. Hebrews 4:12

Satan is a liar. John 8:44

God will make a way. Isaiah 43:18–19

God's Word will accomplish God's purposes. Isaiah 55:11–12

You can pray with confidence. John 15:7

Commit the Word to memory: Get yourself a stack of sticky notes. Print God's Word on those notes and post them all over your house. Read the Word aloud and allow the truth to penetrate your soul.

Chapter Fourteen

Why I Have Nothing to Fear

> So do not fear, for I am with you; do not be dismayed, for I am your God. I will strengthen you and help you; I will uphold you with my righteous right hand.
>
> Isaiah 41:10

In the introduction to this book, I told you how I was afraid to approach the subject of spiritual warfare for fear of what the devil might do to me. I also warned you in chapter 2 that if you were afraid you should perhaps put this book away and read another one. But now that you've made it this far, I want to congratulate you. Where you might have once been ignorant, you aren't stupid (and you're not as ignorant as you once were either). Today you are on to Satan. You know who he is and what he is capable of doing. You know a bit about his conniving spirit and the way he unleashes his attacks on you. You are armed and dangerous.

In this chapter, you will collect five smooth stones to add to your arsenal. By the time you finish reading this book, I want this to become your war cry: "I'm a woman of God, I've got five smooth stones, and I'm not afraid to use them!"

FIVE SMOOTH STONES

If I had been sitting on the riverbank when David went to choose his stones, I would have loved to have asked him how he was able to muster such faith. I wonder if his mother read him God's Word from cover to cover (like I did for TJ when he was four years old). I wonder if while he was spending hours alone in the pastures God impressed him with His glory through nature. I wonder if David and his father talked for hours in the night about life and death and war and peace. I wonder why he chose *five* smooth stones—it only took one!

Before you read any more, go collect five rocks. I have five rocks piled on my desk and five more on the end table next to my couch. Many times I collect five rocks to remind me of the following truths. My stones serve as little altars to remind me that with God's power coursing through my veins I will win every battle I fight.

Do you have your rocks? If so, then read on and learn more about the stones God's given you to take your giants down.

THE STONE OF CONTENTMENT

If we could learn to find our satisfaction in Christ alone, we would withstand so much of what the Enemy hurls our way. Many times I allow Satan an edge in my marriage because I grow discontent with my husband. Is it just me, or have you ever thought, "If only I'd never met you!" I knew I loved Ruth Graham when I heard this story about her. She said that early on in her marriage, before any children were born, Billy moved her to the outskirts of Chicago—away from her friends and family. One day some of his friends visited unannounced and suggested they go into the city. She was eager to go with them, but Billy told her, "No women today." No amount of pleading would change his mind, so as the car drove away she tearfully prayed, "God, if you'll forgive me for marrying him I promise I'll never do it again."[1] Sometimes it seems that if you could just somehow (discreetly) remove that man you married from the face of the earth, all your problems would go away!

But if we were to allow God to take the layers of self-righteousness off our own hearts, we would discover that we're trying to find our satisfaction in our husbands—and there is the problem. When Tom fails to meet my every need, God is using Tom to point me to himself. When Tom disappoints me, God is using Tom to say, "Only I can fill you up!" There is a God-sized hole in each of our hearts, and when we try to fill it with husbands, ministries, careers, hobbies, children, grandchildren, or whatever else, sooner or later we find that they just don't fit. Rather than get upset with them (don't forget that your Enemy is not flesh and blood), run to your Savior and find contentment in Him.

David was able to take Goliath down because he found his contentment in God. While his brothers might have found their contentment in being soldiers of Saul, David found his contentment in God. David's brothers thought he was just a shepherd boy. While they went off to the battle, David obediently tended the sheep. Most likely David wanted to be in the action of battle—most likely he couldn't wait to get there. But David stayed behind under the authority of his father and waited to go to the battlefield when his father sent him.

Oh, that we would do the same. What battles we might win if we truly found our contentment in Christ alone. To hurl your stone of contentment at the giant that heckles you, you must rest secure in the "whoevers" God sees fit to put in (and take out of) your life and the "wherevers" He sees fit to place you in His great big world (both geographic and circumstantial locations).

Consider your stone of contentment and pray this prayer aloud:

Father God, I choose to place my hope in you. I release (whomever you run to when you need God) from having to meet my every need. I confess that I've allowed (him/her) to take your place in my life. Please forgive me for doing that. I choose you—because you chose me. I trust you, I love you, and I am satisfied with you. Amen.

THE STONE OF CONFIDENCE

Oh, this is a big one for me: *confidence*. I used to think I had to rally confidence and self-esteem in me. Remember Satan's intimidation factor? When David faced Goliath, was he confident in himself? Or was His confidence in God?

When Saul insisted that David wear the king's armor, David tried it on and then refused. After arming himself with a slingshot and five smooth stones, David stood before Goliath and exposed himself to Goliath's verbal assault.

> He said to David, "Am I a dog, that you come at me with sticks?" And the Philistine cursed David by his gods. "Come here," he said, "and I'll give your flesh to the birds of the air and the beasts of the field!"
>
> David said to the Philistine, "You come against me with sword and spear and javelin, but I come against you in the name of the Lord Almighty, the God of the armies of Israel, whom you have defied. This day the Lord will hand you over to me, and I'll strike you down and cut off your head."
>
> 1 SAMUEL 17:43–46

Where was David's confidence? How long has it been since you've witnessed the power of God? When's the last time you saw His power demonstrated? What is God able to do? According to His Word, nothing is too difficult for God: "Ah Lord God! Behold, You have made the heavens and the earth by Your great power and by Your outstretched arm! Nothing is too difficult for You!" (Jeremiah 32:17 NASB).

Jeremiah also reminds us that we are blessed when we choose to trust God: "Blessed is the man who trusts in the Lord, whose confidence is in him" (Jeremiah 17:7).

And you certainly want to remember that God promises to meet every one of your needs: "My God shall supply all your need according to his riches in glory by Christ Jesus" (Philippians 4:19 KJV).

Where is your confidence today? Hold your confidence stone in the palm of your hand and say this prayer with me:

Lord, I confess that I've been hiding in my tent afraid because the Enemy is strong. I choose to believe that you alone are God. I choose to believe that there is "nothing too difficult for you." No giant too big, no problem too large, no child too lost, no marriage too cold, no church too mean, (add anything that comes to your mind). For nothing is too difficult for you. I choose to trust you. I have made you my hope and my confidence. I trust you to supply all that I need. Amen.

THE STONE OF PERSEVERANCE

So many times this statement is true: We win because we refuse to quit. Tom reminds me often that our journey in God's kingdom work is a marathon, not a sprint. Our evangelism pastor, Steve Witt, challenged me one night when he asked a group of us this question: "Is there any quit in you?" He went on to say, "If there is, you can be sure the devil's gonna find it, and he's gonna camp out there until you give in."

When I heard Steve ask that question, I had been guilty of both thinking and speaking these words aloud: "I can't. It's too much. I've had enough. I can't go on. . . ."

I think the devil heard those comments of defeat and they were like a "come and get it!" cry for him to mess with me. "Leighann's down! She's discouraged, her hope is fading, her faith is waning—let's go poke her in the belly and see if we can get a wound to fester!" he and his demons shouted.

In case you haven't noticed, the devil is not nice at all. If you have a place in your heart that's still harboring resentment or bitterness, it's like a gaping wound begging him to come and infect it. If you have a relationship that is strained, a dream that seems to be hopeless, or a doubt that nags you, then these heartaches create spotlights for your weaknesses. They shout, "Chink in the armor! She's got a leak! Come on, fellas—let's see what we can do!"

Is there any quit in you? When Steve asked that question, I had served Thompson Station Church alongside my husband for fifteen years. We had grown from eight to over one thousand people in attendance. I'd seen many people rise to places of leadership in our church, and I'd had fallouts with some of them. I'd enjoyed friendships with some and suffered broken confidences with others. I had experienced both success and failure in the ministry. I've now served the Lord through church for more than twenty years, and I've held a baby while we buried his mother and I've wrapped my arms around other mothers while we buried their babies. I have been blessed with tremendous answered prayers, and I have experienced moments in my partnership with my husband and in my relationship with my children that went beyond words in their depth of joy.

I got to thinking that night that Steve challenged me, and I realized, "No, there's not any quit in me." This was a brand-new revelation. Deep passion began to stir in my spirit, and I heard my heart stand up and shout, "I'm going to serve, I'm going to live, I'm going to give, I'm going to grow—and forgetting what lies behind I'm going to press on!"

What about you? Consider your stone of perseverance and pray this prayer aloud:

Father, I do not want to grow weary doing good. But I'm tired. I've already grown weary, and sometimes I think I just might quit. I too have been guilty of thinking—if not saying—"I've had enough!" But here I am, Lord. I choose to follow you and I don't intend to give up. There's no quit in me. Did you hear that, Satan? There's no quit in me! I love you, Lord . . . and forgetting what lies behind . . . I press on. Amen.

THE STONE OF FAITH

I think this stone is the stone David pulled from his bag of five to bring Goliath down. David's faith was compacted into that one stone. And that faith-stone, partnered with David's arm of obedience, took down the Philistine giant that had God's entire army held captive in their tents. Oh, that God's people would hurl such faith today! The world is desperately hungry to experience faith like that. People want to know . . . is your God real?

We have incredible power to proclaim the name of the Lord as we face our Goliaths. If you've ever been snow skiing, you know that the most difficult trails are marked with black diamonds. Although I enjoy skiing, I've no need to experience the adrenaline rush of those hazardous trails. In my book *Women Embracing Life . . . All of It!* I use my experience with snow skiing to illustrate how the world watches to see God's children navigate the difficult, mogul-infested slopes of life. Even though most of us would rather stay on the bunny hill, sometimes God leads us to the black diamond trails.

But why wouldn't God lead us there? God's people (and our lost neighbors and friends) need to see what happens when our lives embrace the promises of God. They desperately need to see that God is personal and that He is powerful. The world needs to see that with our faith we can move mountains. They need to understand that God is real and His power is sufficient!

Even when we fall down, we will get up again and march triumphantly on! Don't forget that this stone is not optional. Hebrews 11:6 says, "And without faith it is impossible to please God, because anyone who comes to him must believe that he exists and that he rewards those that earnestly seek him."

There is an interesting word in that verse: *earnestly*. How do we earnestly seek God? To seek God earnestly means to seek Him with the confidence that "those who seek me with their whole heart will find me!" (see Jeremiah 29:13). To seek God earnestly means to keep on seeking Him when everything around you says, "What's the point?" Faith is the extra measure of *umph* that refuses to give up, give in, or give out.

Hold the powerful stone of faith and pray this prayer:

> *Oh, God, enlarge faith in us! We want to PLEASE you—your reward is what we long for! Father, let our earnestness be proven in the winds of doubt. And our faith strengthened as we cling tenaciously to your Word.*

THE STONE OF INTIMACY WITH GOD

There is really only one way to defeat the Enemy—and that is to nurture your personal relationship with the only One who is stronger, and that is God. I love a good story, and Max Lucado tells one that describes this stone perfectly, so let me retell it here.

In Max Lucado's children's book *The Song of the King*, the king offers his daughter in marriage to the knight who can survive the Hemlock Forest. The Hemlock Forest is a dark and fearsome place filled with hope-nots who heckle and attack strangers who dare to enter their forest.

Three knights enter the contest, and each of them is given the opportunity to choose one traveling companion before they take off on their journey. When the brave and gallant knights ask how they will find their way out of the forest and back to the king in the castle, they are told that the king will play his flute at the end of each day. They are simply to follow the sound of the song.

There were only two people who knew the song of the king. Those people were the king and his son, the crown prince of the kingdom.

The three knights chose their traveling companions and took off on their fearsome journey. After many long days only one returned. A great banquet was prepared in his honor, and he spent the evening telling of all the great adventures in the Hemlock Forest. Of all the dangers he encountered, he told his captive audience that the worst was that the hope-nots learned to mimic the song of the king.

Each evening when the king played his tune, melodies arose from all parts of the forest. The knight admitted that this would have been his undoing had he not chosen his traveling companion wisely. At this moment, the knight's traveling companion was revealed. He was . . . the king's own son, the crown prince of the kingdom. The brave and wise knight went on to explain that as he spent time with the prince, the prince played him the beloved song, and because he heard the song so often he learned to recognize the *true* song of the king.[2]

My dear sister in the faith—there are powerful forces of evil mimicking the voice of God. They will try to derail you and render you useless to the kingdom of God. Or worse than that, they will use you as a pawn to wreak havoc on God's kingdom with no regard for the destruction they deliver to you, your family, and your friends. In order to guard yourself against their tactics, you too must embrace the song of the king by growing deeply intimate with His Son, Jesus Christ.

Consider your stone of intimacy with God and pray this prayer aloud:

Father, we are quite an army—the few of us. And we're women at that! Steel magnolias . . . we don't feel like we're so strong. But we do love you, and we sense a strong calling to your purpose and your plan. You alone are God, and we place our hope in you. Today, I recommit myself to a deep, personal, intimate relationship with you. I need you, Lord. More than I can even know. Father, I want to continue to be "armed and dangerous." I want to put the Enemy on the run and take every giant down so the world will know you are God. Amen.

Why I Have Nothing to Fear

Reconsider each of your five smooth stones. Ask yourself these questions:

The stone of contentment: Am I satisfied "In Christ alone"?

The stone of confidence: Do I trust God?

The stone of faith: Do I really believe that God is able?

The stone of perseverance: Is there any quit in me?

The stone of intimacy with God: Do I love the Lord my God with all my heart, strength, mind, and soul?

Go back and pray the prayers again.

SHARPEN YOUR SWORD

God is with you. Isaiah 41:10

Is anything too difficult for God? No! Genesis 18:14 and Jeremiah 32:17

God is your confidence. Jeremiah 17:7

Without faith it is impossible to please God. Hebrews 11:6

Apart from Christ we can do nothing. John 15:5

Commit the Word to memory: Consider one verse from this book that could be a life verse for you right now. Print it on a tiny slip of paper and place it in a locket (or one of those little prayer box necklaces). Repeat the verse often.

A BLESSING TO CLOSE

I have a dear friend, Karen, who might be the most faith-filled believer I've ever met. She is also one of the most positive people in the world. (I would imagine her faith and her positive nature are intertwined with one another.) When I spend time with Karen, my spirit is lifted and my heart soars. I want to close this book with one of her blessings. It is a blessing of peace. For now that you have read this book, you can walk with your head held high, your sword drawn, and your mind at peace.

> *Jesus gave His peace to the disciples before He left them. Today, I pray a blessing upon you with the peace of Jesus which is beyond anything the world can give you. His peace transcends all other things that come against you, having total rest, assurance, comfort, trusting calmness, and complete peace.*
>
> *I bless you with the peace He had of being in the right place at the right time, living with the urgency of His purpose within himself without being overwhelmed by fear or anxiety from that urgency, because He knew His Father's time was perfect.*
>
> *I speak a blessing over you today to be peaceful because you know ahead of time that your Father God will partner with you to provide adequacy for each day, whether a day with pain or pleasure.*
>
> *I speak this blessing upon you in the name of Jesus, who wants you to be in perfect peace with Him!*
>
> *Amen.*

A Word to My Readers

As I was dotting my i's and crossing my t's, I thought to myself, "What would I have written in this book had I not been diagnosed with cancer, had my church not been flooded, and had my daughter not left home so abruptly?" I smile as I ponder that thought. When Ron (my manager) sent my book proposal to Bethany House, I had a good idea for writing a book on spiritual warfare. I outlined my plans and presented my thesis. But the book you've read is very different from the one I had in mind to write. The difference was made because God allowed me to write from the trenches of a messy battlefield.

Today I'm finishing my part of this book and preparing to attach it to an e-mail and turn it in to my publisher. Last week I posted this on my Facebook page: "Am completing my final edit and preparing to send my book to the publisher. I feel the earth shake under my feet. There will be shouts of 'hallelujah' coming from our house next Wednesday!" My son was the first to comment. He wrote this: "Seriously!"

My whole family is ready for this project to be over. I'm tired, a bit wounded, and somewhat tattered from the experience. You know the three big battles I've fought, but there have also been little aggravating skirmishes in between those. Last week (just two weeks prior to my deadline) my entire book was lost on my computer. Andrew, our IT guy who takes care of our church's system, told me that there was absolutely no explanation for this. He was baffled. Fortunately, I'd made a hard copy a few weeks ago so that I could do some editing while I was out of town. For a day one paper copy of this manuscript was all that I had. I thank God I had that one!

In the process of putting my manuscript back into the computer, I was convinced that two chapters (13 and 14) were completely *lost*. If you write, you know what I mean when I say they were lost. For when I have a book in my head it is like a pregnancy—that book is *in there*. But once I print it on the computer it's out! Kind of like giving birth; there's no going back. When I thought my chapters were lost, I begged God to give me back the thoughts that I'd had before I "birthed" them. On the day I started writing a new chapter 13 (laboring to give birth to something that wasn't really there), I hit "save" and my computer asked me if I wanted to replace the old chapter 13 with the new one. That was when I discovered that chapters 13 and 14 were not lost after all.

In the midst of that crisis our air-conditioner went out in both our house and my office (which is above a detached garage). The wireless Internet we have in our home is not really strong enough to work without slipping us in and out of service, so I pressed through that inconvenience, and my computer is still suffering a "bug" as it freezes for two minutes each time I open or close a file. A few weeks ago I almost fell down a flight of stairs. Fortunately I caught myself, but I injured my thumb. So I've been typing this month with a brace on my left hand (and even now my arm is all tingly from the injury). In the past month Tom and I have paid for two cars that were towed, once for each of our daughters. I won't bore you with the details—just know that having our cars towed is not something that happens often.

Enough of my whining. I just want you to know that even with these aggravating skirmishes and in the midst of the major battles, I am convinced more than ever that God is good. I am smiling today, for I know by experience what God's love does. He's going to win the battle I'm engaged in this minute because He is the Lord Almighty and I am His beloved daughter. I hope that, no matter what you are facing this moment, you know (in your knower) that this is true:

Every attack from the Enemy brings with it a divine invitation from the sovereign hand of God to learn by *experience* what love does.

You have already won!

Notes

Introduction

1. Anna B. Warner, "Jesus Loves Me," 1860.

Part One: The Most Powerful Weapon of All—the Love of God

1. Chip Ingram, *The Invisible War: What Every Believer Needs to Know About Satan, Demons, and Spiritual Warfare* (Grand Rapids, MI: Baker Books, 2006), 71.

Chapter Two: What Love Does

1. Buryl Red and Grace Hawthorne, *It's Cool in the Furnace* (Nashville: Word Music, 1975).

2. Each pastor at our church has a group of prayer partners. I have seven women who are committed to praying for me. We meet once a month to pray together. I encourage you to participate in a prayer partnership with two or more women.

Chapter Three: Love's Completed Work

1. George Bennard, "The Old Rugged Cross," 1913.

2. Elvina M. Hall, "Jesus Paid It All," 1865.

3. John Newton, "Amazing Grace," 1779.

4. Ibid., "When we've been there" verse by unknown, 1829.

5. Ibid.

Part Two: The Enemy Exposed

1. Beth Moore, *Praying God's Word* (Nashville: Broadman and Holman, 2000), 4.

Chapter Four: Spiritual Warfare Is Real

1. Chuck Lawless, *Giving Ourselves to Prayer* (Terre Haute, IN: Prayer Shop, 2008), 470.

2. E. M. Bounds, *E. M. Bounds on Prayer* (New Kensington, PA: Whitaker House, 1997), 167.

Chapter Five: Who My Enemy Is

1. Millard Erickson, *Christian Theology* (Grand Rapids, MI: Baker Book House, 1983), vol. 1, 433–451.

2. Ibid.

3. Ibid.

4. Ibid., 448.

5. Neil T. Anderson, *The Bondage Breaker* (Eugene, OR: Harvest House, 2000), 166.

6. Nancy Leigh DeMoss, *Lies Women Believe and the Truth That Sets Them Free* (Chicago: Moody Press, 2001), table of contents.

7. John Bevere, *The Bait of Satan* (Orlando: Creation House, 1994), 9–10.

Chapter Six: What My Enemy Does

1. Beth Moore, *Praying God's Word* (Nashville: Broadman and Holman, 2000), 4.

Part Three: The Targets in Our Lives

1. E. M. Bounds, *Guide to Spiritual Warfare* (New Kensington, PA: Whitaker House, 1984), 97–98.

Chapter Seven: Satan Targets My Marriage

1. Amy Desai, "Who Gets Divorced?" *Should I Get a Divorce? Things You Should Know Before You Call the Attorney* (Colorado Springs: Focus on the Family, 2006), http://www.focusonthefamily.com/marriage/divorce_and_infidelity/should_i_get_a_divorce/who_gets_divorced.aspx.

2. David Popenoe and Barbara Dafoe Whitehead, *The State of Our Unions 2001*, National Marriage Project, Rutgers, June 2001, p. 21, http://www.virginia.edu/marriageproject/.

3. Ibid., pp. 18, 20.

4. Glenn T. Stanton, *Why Marriage Matters: Reasons to Believe in Marriage in Postmodern Society* (Colorado Springs: Pinon Press, 1997), p. 29; Judith Wallerstein, et al., *The Unexpected Legacy of Divorce: A 25 Year Landmark Study* (New York: Hyperion, 2000), p. xxvi.

5. "Christians Are More Likely to Experience Divorce Than Are Non-Christians," Barna Research Group, December 21, 2000, barna.org.

6. Shaunti Feldhahn, "Commitment," *Focus on the Family*, January 2009, http://www.focusonthefamily.com/marriage/strengthening_your_marriage/commitment.aspx.

7. Charles Stanley, *When the Enemy Strikes* (Nashville: Thomas Nelson, 2004), 99.

8. Ibid., 100.

Chapter Nine: Satan Targets My Friendships With Other Women

1. Anderson, 223.

2. Stuart Briscoe, *David: A Heart for God* (Wheaton, IL: Victor Books, 1984), 70.

3. Anderson, 225.

Chapter Eleven: Satan Targets My Church

1. Tim Bowman, "What's a 'Significant' Ministry?" *Leadership Journal*, June 22, 2004, http://www.ctlibrary.com/le/currenttrendscolumns/leadershipweekly/cln40622.html.

2. Ibid.

Part Four: Victory Is Mine

1. Jerry Rankin, *Spiritual Warfare: The Battle for God's Glory* (Nashville: B&H Books, 2009), 32.

Chapter Twelve: Who I Am in Christ

1. Anderson, 11.

2. Adapted from Leighann McCoy, *Women Touched by Jesus* (Houston: Freeman-Smith, 2009). Used by permission.

3. Grady Nutt, *Being Me: Self, You Bug Me* (Nashville: Broadman Press, 1971), 11.

4. Helen H. Lemmel, "Turn Your Eyes Upon Jesus," 1922.

5. Nutt, 76–78.

6. Warner.

Chapter Thirteen: How I Defeat My Enemy

1. Rankin, 8.

2. Ron Hutchcraft, "The Prize and the Prison," *A Word With You*, #6021, February 8, 2010, http://www.hutchcraft.com/a-word-with-you/your-hindrances/the-prize-and-the-prison-6021.

3. William Barclay, *Flesh and Spirit* (Grand Rapids, MI: Baker Book House, 1976), 19–20.

4. Ibid., 21–22.

5. Jennifer Kennedy Dean, *The Life-Changing Power in the Blood of Christ* (Birmingham, AL: New Hope Publishers, 2003).

6. Jim Cromarty, *It Is Not Death to Die: A New Biography of Hudson Taylor* (Fearn, Ross-shire, Scotland: Christian Focus Publications, 2008), 366.

Chapter Fourteen: Why I Have Nothing to Fear

1. Patricia Daniels Cornwell, *Ruth, A Portrait: The Story of Ruth Bell Graham* (New York: Doubleday, 1998), 100.

2. Max Lucado, *The Song of the King* (Wheaton, IL: Crossway Books, 1995).

Bibliography

Anderson, Neil T. *The Bondage Breaker*. Eugene, OR: Harvest House, 2000.

Barclay, William. *Flesh and Spirit: An Examination of Galatians 5:19–23*. Grand Rapids, MI: Baker Book House, 1976.

Bevere, John. *The Bait of Satan: Your Response Determines Your Future*. Orlando: Creation House, 1994.

Bounds, Edward M. E. M. *Bounds on Prayer*. New Kensington, PA: Whitaker House, 1997.

Bounds, Edward M. *Guide to Spiritual Warfare*. New Kensington, PA: Whitaker House, 1984.

Briscoe, D. Stuart. *David: A Heart for God*. Wheaton, IL: Victor, 1984.

Clark, Jerusha. *Every Thought Captive: Battling the Toxic Beliefs That Separate Us from the Life We Crave*. Colorado Springs: TH1NK, 2006.

Crawford, Dan R. *Giving Ourselves to Prayer: An Acts 6:4 Primer for Ministry*. Terre Haute, IN: PrayerShop, 2008.

Cromarty, Jim. *It Is Not Death to Die: A New Biography of Hudson Taylor*. Fearn, Ross-shire, Scotland: Christian Focus, 2008.

Dean, Jennifer Kennedy. *The Life-Changing Power in the Blood of Christ*. Birmingham, AL: New Hope, 2003.

DeMoss, Nancy Leigh. *Lies Women Believe: And the Truth That Sets Them Free*. Chicago: Moody, 2001.

Erickson, Millard J. *Christian Theology*. Vol. 1. Grand Rapids, MI: Baker, 1983.

Ingram, Chip. *The Invisible War: What Every Believer Needs to Know About Satan, Demons, and Spiritual Warfare*. Grand Rapids, MI: Baker, 2006.

Lewis, C. S. *The Screwtape Letters: With Screwtape Proposes a Toast*. San Francisco: HarperSanFrancisco, 2001.

Lucado, Max, and Toni Goffe. *The Song of the King*. Wheaton, IL: Crossway, 1995.

Moore, Beth. *Praying God's Word: Breaking Free From Spiritual Strongholds*. Nashville: Broadman & Holman, 2000.

Nutt, Grady. *Being Me*. Nashville: Broadman Press, 1971.

Rankin, Jerry. *Spiritual Warfare: The Battle for God's Glory*. Nashville: B&H Books, 2009.

Stanley, Charles F. *When the Enemy Strikes: The Keys to Winning Your Spiritual Battles*. Nashville: Nelson, 2004.

About the Author

Leighann McCoy is a sought-after speaker and writer. She is the prayer and women's minister at a large Southern Baptist church where her husband serves as pastor. She has written a number of devotionals and Bible studies for women. She and her husband have three children and one grandchild. They live in Franklin, Tennessee.